PERSPECTIVES AND IRONY
IN AMERICAN SLAVERY

Perspectives and Irony in American Slavery

Essays by
CARL N. DEGLER
EUGENE D. GENOVESE
DAVID BRION DAVIS
STANLEY L. ENGERMAN
WILLIAM K. SCARBOROUGH
JOHN W. BLASSINGAME
KENNETH M. STAMPP

Edited by
HARRY P. OWENS

UNIVERSITY PRESS OF MISSISSIPPI
JACKSON
1976

Copyright © 1976 by the
University Press of Mississippi
Manufactured in the United States of America
First printing: September, 1976
Second printing: June, 1977

Library of Congress Cataloging in Publication Data
Main entry under title:

Perspectives and irony in American slavery.

Papers presented at a conference organized by the
Dept. of History of the University of Mississippi and
held Oct. 1975.
Bibliography: p.
1. Slavery in the United States—Congresses.
I. Degler, Carl N.   II. Owens, Harry P.   III. Mississippi.
University. Dept. of History.
E441.P47   301.44′93′0973   76–18283
ISBN 0–87805–074–4
ISBN 0–87805–025–6 pbk.

THIS VOLUME IS SPONSORED BY THE
UNIVERSITY OF MISSISSIPPI

The Department of History
of the University of Mississippi
respectfully dedicates
this volume
to
CLARE L. MARQUETTE
Colleague and Scholar

Contents

Introduction

Few institutions have influenced American history as much as
slavery. Chattel slavery, existing in North America from the mid-
seventeenth through the mid-nineteenth centuries, produced
immense wealth for the planter class, poverty and economic stagnation for many non-slaveowning southerners, raw materials for
the industrial revolution, extreme stress and conflict concerning
the social, intellectual, and religious ideals of Americans, and
untold hardships and anguish for millions of men, women, and
children of African descent. Its abolition cost the lives of more than
600,000 Americans during a devastating civil war which was followed by an effort to expand the Constitution of the United States
to include black Americans—an effort that had to be repeated a
hundred years later. And yet vestiges of the peculiar institution
remain.

Slavery existed for more than 200 years; it has been more than a
century since the Thirteenth Amendment was ratified. For at least
three centuries, slavery has generated discussion, heated debate,
or active denunciation. The fact that scholars continue to debate
slavery attests to its significance as a formidable institution in
shaping America. It is part of the irony of slavery that historians
studying the institution for almost a century have failed to provide
all the answers; indeed, perhaps they have not yet asked all the
right questions. Even more frustrating is the probability that they
will not be able to do so.

The complexity of the institution, the scarcity of source materials, the increasingly more sophisticated methodologies, and the more subtle conceptualizations raise questions in geometric rather than arithmetic progression. The sheer number of people who lived in slavery, the variety of physical conditions under which they lived, the psychological proclivities of individual slaveholders, the ability of slaves to respond to their peculiar circumstances, and the arguments and counterarguments of human versus property rights created such complex relationships and ever-changing situations that historians constantly face the problems of interpreting the evidence. Most generalizations tend to be so riddled with exceptions as to require further examination. Even with the insights of the behavioral scientists and the sophisticated methodology of the cliometricians (some would say because of), more questions are raised than answers given. But, after all, that is one of the major purposes of scholarship. Professor Kenneth M. Stampp, in his essay "Slavery—The Historian's Burden," warns that students of slavery should not expect a definitive study, nor even consensus except on a limited number of issues. If a definitive study is impossible and consensus improbable, then students of slavery need a perspective. The essays in this volume represent the considered judgment of major scholars of slavery. They offer, not consensus, but seven perspectives which range from Eugene D. Genovese's interpretation as seen from a world view to John W. Blassingame's paper reflecting the slaves' view of their community.

While the American Revolution Bicentennial was being planned in 1974–75, and soon after publication of three major studies on slavery—*Time on the Cross* by Robert W. Fogel and Stanley L. Engerman, David Brion Davis' *The Problem of Slavery in the Age of Revolution, 1770–1823*, and Eugene D. Genovese's *Roll, Jordan, Roll: The World the Slaves Made*—a colleague in the Department of History, David G. Sansing, proposed that the department offer a symposium on slavery. Believing that the time, the place, and the topic had come together, the Department of

History of the University of Mississippi began to prepare for the three-day conference that was held in October, 1975.

The department's symposium committee selected the title "The Slave Experience in America: A Bicentennial Perspective," and proposed seven very general topics. The seven speakers who agreed to present papers were given only a broad outline of the symposium, so they could develop their papers without limitations. When the speakers arrived at the University of Mississippi they found that a common theme had developed independently. This theme was established by Professor Carl N. Degler in his paper "The Irony of American Negro Slavery." With grateful acknowledgment to Professor Degler and to the subsequent speakers who expanded on the theme, the Department of History offers *Perspectives and Irony in American Slavery.* We are indeed grateful for the contributions of each author, and it is only fair to note that they were not asked to present fully documented papers. For those who chose to footnote their papers, we are pleased to publish them as presented.

Other scholars were invited to introduce the speaker of each session, to comment on the papers if they so desired, and to conduct the discussions. These moderators deserve special commendations for their remarks and abilities in handling the discussion periods. Professor Margaret Walker Alexander of Jackson State University helped establish the mood of the symposium by introducing the first speaker, Carl N. Degler. Professor Richard N. Current, president of the Southern Historical Association, served as moderator for Eugene D. Genovese, while Dr. R. A. McLemore introduced William K. Scarborough. One of the more prolific writers in black history, Professor Benjamin Quarles, presided during the session in which John W. Blassingame offered new interpretations of the slave community. Professor John H. Moore, formerly of the University of Mississippi but now with The Florida State University, introduced Stanley L. Engerman. Professor Winthrop D. Jordan presided during David Brion Davis' presentation, and Professor Glover Moore concluded the program by introducing Kenneth M. Stampp. The success of the symposium was to a large degree due to the contributions of these scholars, and we extend to them our warmest thanks.

In an undertaking of this nature we cannot but express our appreciation to those who helped in many different ways. To the Rust College A Cappella Choir, under the direction of Charles Holmes, we offer special thanks for their musical presentation "Tribute to a Heritage." We gratefully acknowledge a grant from the Mississippi American Revolution Bicentennial Commission, a travel grant from the American Council of Learned Societies, and support offered by the University of Mississippi Foundation. We wish to express our special appreciation to Dr. Porter L. Fortune, Chancellor of the University of Mississippi, Dr. Arthur H. De-Rosier, Vice-Chancellor for Academic Affairs, Dr. Joseph Sam, Dean of the Graduate School, and Dr. M. B. Huneycutt, Dean of the College of Liberal Arts, for their continuing moral and administrative support. We wish to thank Professor William K. Scarborough for his suggestions during the early planning stages. We appreciate the efforts of the University of Mississippi Division of Continuing Education for surmounting so many of the logistical problems. Commendations are offered to all members of the department, who gave so unsparingly of their time and energy.

HARRY P. OWENS
University of Mississippi
Oxford, Mississippi

PERSPECTIVES AND IRONY
IN AMERICAN SLAVERY

The Irony
of American Negro Slavery

CARL N. DEGLER

All Americans, black as well as white, northerners as well as southerners, must be struck by the irony of slavery in the history of their country. One dictionary defines irony as "a situation, a turn of events which frustrates and appears to mock the hopes or aims of human beings; a result opposite to what might be expected." Even before there was a United States, Dr. Johnson, the English Tory, noted the irony of slavery when he asked, "How is it that we hear the loudest *yelps* for liberty among the drivers of negroes?"

The conflict between human bondage and the phrase "all men are created equal" in the Revolution's great Declaration must have been too direct for all to ignore, for at least some slaveholders reacted to the cruel irony by freeing their slaves. Yet the contradiction was not great enough to move most, and so the irony persisted. Americans boasted of their social order as one of freedom, while ignoring slavery. John C. Calhoun announced to the world that the leaders of the United States "are charged by Providence not only with the happiness of this great people, but with that of the human race. We have a government of a new order . . . founded on the rights of man, resting on . . . reason."

Nor was the irony only to be found in the fact that both Calhoun and the author of the Declaration of Independence were slaveholders, for slavery as it developed in the United States was more than the antithesis of freedom. It denied freedom to a particular group of people, thereby not only ignoring the precepts

3

of individual freedom but also denying the equality of all people. Only some men and women, those with black skins, were slaves. For as Duncan MacLeod has shown, when Americans could not reconcile their revolutionary principle of political freedom with the institution of slavery, they kept their philosophy *and* slavery by redefining the humanity of the Negro. To a liberal of the nineteenth century like John Stuart Mill, the United States was "a country where institutions profess to be founded on equality and which yet maintain the slavery of black men."

Another foreign observer, Alexis de Tocqueville, was also disturbed by the irony to which slavery and equality gave birth in the United States. He felt that "the prejudice of race appears to be stronger in the states that have abolished slavery than in those states where it still exists; and nowhere is it so intolerant as in those states where servitude has never been known." Tocqueville was referring, of course, to the middle western states of his day, where the Northwest Ordinance had forbidden slavery from the outset, yet where some of the most stringent laws against blacks were to be found. The fact that the new Republic of the West should also be the most populous slave society in history is only the beginning of the ironies that run through the history of slavery in the United States. Slavery and the American experience are intertwined; what one is, the other helped to create.

At few times in the history of slavery is irony more evident than in regard to the closing of the slave trade on January 1, 1808. Among the reasons for the constitutional provision that permitted the closing was the intention to limit the extent of slavery, if not to end the institution itself, in the United States. James Wilson in the Pennsylvania ratifying convention asserted, "I consider this as laying the foundation for banishing slavery out of this country." And even when one acknowledges that the motives for putting the clause in the Constitution were mixed, as W. E. B. Du Bois wrote, "there was still discernible a certain underlying agreement in the dislike of slavery." It seems ironical, too, that the one slave society which required a civil war to rid itself of slavery should have been the second to close for good the African slave trade. Only Denmark preceded the United States in this action. Even Great Britain, whose cruisers during the nineteenth century would relentlessly pursue slavers over the South Atlantic, did not finally end the infamous traffic until several months after the United States Congress had made its position clear in March, 1807. The irony mounts further when it is remembered that the outlawing of the slave trade was achieved in Britain at a time when only a few dozen West Indian slaveholders sat in Parliament, while in the United States the deed was accomplished when almost half the members of Congress and even the president were themselves slaveholders or representatives of slaveholding constituencies.

There is evidence, too, that the motives behind the closing of the slave trade were not only mixed, but racist as well. The fact that all the southern slave states had closed the trade at one time or another before the federal government acted suggests that the desire to maintain a white man's country may have been as influential as the concern to end an inhumane traffic. Yet even if the motives were less noble than tradition would like, the ending of the trade was certainly a gain for blacks and for humanity.

Even so, irony remains, because America's closing of the slave trade earlier than any other major slave society fostered developments that fastened slavery more firmly upon the South. Because no more slaves could be imported from Africa, the price of bondsmen escalated in the face of the rising demand for slaves to open and settle the fresh lands of the Southwest. Those planters or slaveholders who lived in areas where slave labor was not as useful as in the past, such as in Virginia and South Carolina, now found their human property growing in value. Their interest in the perpetuation of the institution was to that extent enhanced. Moreover, each new western investor in slaves found himself tied to the institution by an ever-increasing financial commitment. Manumission, too, was made more difficult by a high price for slaves, because the financial sacrifice required to effect it was to that extent increased.

A rise in the financial commitment to slavery was not the only way in which the closing of the slave trade tightened the grip of slavery on the United States. Once the decision was made to rely upon reproduction for replenishing the supply of slaves, the conditions of slavery had to be made conducive to the bearing and rearing of young slaves to maturity. Whether the decision was as rational as here implied is not really material. It is possible that the slave trade was able to be closed only because natural increase had already demonstrated that it was capable of meeting the demand for new slaves. The source of the decision, however, is not as important as the fact that the exigencies of maintaining a slave system without additions from outside the country were such that the physical condition of the slaves had to be more than minimal. And from present knowledge of the law and the actual treatment of slaves in the colonial period and in the years of the nineteenth century after the closing of the slave trade, conditions did improve markedly, if gradually.

Moreover, if one compares the lot of slaves in the United States with those in Brazil, where the slave trade was not closed effectively until the second half of the nineteenth century, the contrast is striking. In Brazil, slaves were commonly compelled to wear iron masks to control their consumption of alcohol and to prevent them from eating clay, a punishment almost unknown in the United States though the same offenses were common in both societies. (Clay-eating was a means of suicide.) Late in the history of Brazilian slavery, masters were still prone to manumit their old and infirm slaves in order to escape having to care for them. In the United States not even the abolitionists accused the southern slaveholders of such callous behavior.

Perhaps the most persuasive evidence that the closing of the slave trade resulted in an improvement in the lot of the slave was the ability of southern slaveholders to augment continuously their supply of slaves by natural reproduction alone. From the closing of the slave trade right down to 1860, the census revealed that the average yearly increase of the slave population was around 2.5

percent. No other slave society in the New World was able to match this performance, though Barbados apparently managed to maintain its supply through natural reproduction after the closing of the African trade. A somewhat typical pattern in the slave societies of the New World seemed to emerge—once the slave trade was closed the institution of slavery entered upon a decline. The United States, however, proved the exception, for there slavery expanded and grew as never before *after* the African trade was ended. What some had thought was the opening of the road to freedom—the founding fathers, it will be recalled, even refused to use the word "slave" in the Constitution so that future generations would not be reminded of the institution when it was gone— turned out to be the beginning of a new life for slavery.

The expansion and growth of slavery in the United States is ironic in another way. As recently as the 1930s, that school of historians called Civil War revisionists argued that slavery, despite its expansion in the years of the Cotton Kingdom, would have died out in relatively short order if the abolitionists in the North and the proslavery men in the South had not been fanatical in defense of their respective positions. The revisionists contended that slavery was inefficient as a form of labor, and therefore a slave society was not viable. Economics, it was said, in due time would have ended slavery without bloodshed or war.

The irony, of course, is that slavery was hardly a moribund form of labor. It has been shown to be not only an enduring labor system, but one profitable to individual planters as well. The pioneer work of Alfred Conrad and John Meyer almost twenty years ago has been supported by virtually all subsequent inquiries into the subject of the profitability of slaveholding. Conrad and Meyer demonstrated that, on the average, a slaveholder received as good a return on his investment in land and slaves as he would have obtained if he had put his capital in northern securities. In short, rather than seeing the planter as an inefficient producer who limped along with an indifferent labor force because of his love of conspicuous consumption and a need for deferential servants,

historians now must recognize slavery as generally profitable to
the individual planter.

Other investigations have shown that the slave South was expanding not only geographically, but economically as well. Per
capita income rose faster for the slave states between 1840 and
1860 than for the nation at large, and the per capita income of the
new slave states was about what it was for the states of the agricultural Northwest. That computation was made on the basis of slaves
as people; if they are counted as capital, then the per capita income
for all regions of the South outdistances the agricultural free labor
Northwest.

In the light of this recent work, the high price of slaves on the
eve of the Civil War must be read not, as Ulrich B. Phillips
interpreted it, as a danger sign of speculation and overpricing but
as a measure of the demand for slaves and therefore of the expecta-
tion that the continued use of slave labor would bring a good
return. The movement to reopen the slave trade in the late 1850s
must be given a similar interpretation. It was a natural, if abortive,
response to the desire to bring down the price of slaves in a society
that had come to recognize bondage as a way of making money as
well as of making a living.

Slavery, in sum, rather than being an outmoded means of
production that was not likely to survive because it was not making
money for its beneficiaries, actually gave quite solid reasons to
individual planters for endeavoring to keep the institution alive. It
is one of the ironies of southern history that the decision to protect
this institution through secession, as many friends of slavery
pointed out at the time, proved to be the quickest way to overthrow it. For in the absence of outside violence, the future of
slavery was remarkably secure.

One of the reasons for the system's security was its flexibility. At
one time, even those who believed that the return to the planter
was adequate considered slavery as primarily suited, and therefore best confined, to agriculture. Its comparative advantage was
in cotton and the other staples, so the argument went, for these

great staples occupied the slave for the major portion of the year and fitted best his poor work habits derived from the coercion of his labor. But the work of Robert Starobin and others on industrial slavery has since emphasized what knowledge of slavery in other New World societies reinforces. Slavery in practice was a much more adaptable system of labor than its critics then or since have recognized. Starobin showed, for example, that slaves participated in all kinds of industrial and service occupations in the Old South, that they often worked productively side by side with free white workers, and that their skills, when permitted to be developed, were generally on a level with those of free workers. After all, the one manufacturing industry in which the South surpassed the North during the antebellum years—tobacco manufacture—was operated principally by slave labor. The southern iron industry similarly was heavily dependent upon unfree labor. Most recently, John Stealey has shown how slavery made possible a flourishing salt industry in western Virginia that otherwise could not have developed because white labor was too unstable. In that instance, at least, the South gained an industrial enterprise only because of slavery.

Some modern historians have agreed with those antebellum planters who argued that there was a fundamental incompatibility between slavery and the labor needs of manufacturing. These historians have contended that the planters could not condone the threat which industry would pose to the slave system as a whole. The evidence presented in Starobin's book, however, offers little support for this argument. Moreover, as Starobin himself pointed out, planters were actually on both sides of the controversy over the effects of slave labor in factories or of developing industry in the South. Certainly *De Bow's Review* and the several southern commercial conventions did not view with alarm the industrialization in the South. Considering this division on the issue, the matter does not seem to have been a question of class interest in the eyes of the planters. Moreover, to non-slaveholders the use of slaves in non-agricultural pursuits seemed so advantageous to the planters and so threatening to themselves that they often used their power as citizens and voters to prohibit or restrict it. Starobin concluded that "even if slavery is theoretically and practically incompatible in the long run with full industrialization, the point at which this inconsistency would manifest itself had, apparently, not yet been reached between 1790 and 1861. . . . The time when slavery would be absolutely detrimental to southern industries remained quite far off."

In the light of what is now known about the efficiency of slavery, it seems that the failure of the Old South to develop manufacturing is better explained by reference to the comparative advantage of cotton cultivation and its effects upon the economy than to a fundamental incompatibility between slavery as a labor system and industrial development. For the average planter it made more dollars as well as more sense to invest in a plantation and slaves than in manufacturing.

In the nineteenth century, as today, the United States was a leading example of a capitalist society and economy in which individual effort and individual enterprise were central. Yet that same capitalist society was heavily dependent on a form of labor quite outside the individualistic patterns associated with capitalist enterprise. During the years between 1840 and 1860, which were formative in the growth of the modern American economy, the products of slave labor provided the preponderance of the exports of the United States. Right down to 1860, cotton was the nation's largest single export commodity, and the agricultural goods of the slave South consistently made up around 60 percent of the total exports of the United States. These exports, of course, helped to sustain the nation's standard of living and to pay for the imports necessary to bring about the economic growth of those and subsequent years.

Of all the slave societies of the New World, that of the South was the most democratic, both politically and socially. Yet it produced the only frankly racist defense of slavery. All slave societies protected and justified human bondage. Usually the defense was couched in economic terms, often in the name of the protection of the rights of property. Those who stood to lose from the abolition of slavery, whether they lived north or south of the Rio Grande, were always quick to point out how dependent the economy was upon slavery or how essential slaves were in certain crafts or occupations. Very few apologists for slavery outside the United States, however, argued that blacks were racially destined to slavery, as many supporters of slavery in the United States, North and South, contended.

In the United States free white men could participate in government in almost all of the states without reference to property at a time when most free men in Brazil could not vote at all. Ironically enough, it was this very freedom and political power of the ordinary citizen that was a prime source of the peculiarly United States racist defense of slavery. For in a society in which non-slaveholders far outnumbered the slaveholders and at the same time exercised political power, economic self-interest could hardly provide a reliable foundation for the intellectual defense of slavery. In fact, with political power in the hands of the non-slaveholders slavery might well be threatened. Certainly some slaveholders thought so. They seemed to fear the jealousy or the cupidity of the non-slaveholders. It was that fear, for example, that fueled the demand for the reopening of the slave trade in the late 1850s. "The present tendency of supply and demand," wrote one Louisiana editor in 1858, "is to concentrate all the slaves in the hands of the few, and thus excite the envy rather than cultivate the sympathy of the people." If the slave trade were reopened, so the argument ran, then the availability of slaves would increase and the price of slaves would fall. Under such circumstances, one correspondent wrote to a Georgia newspaper, "Where is there a poor man in the South who could not soon become a slaveholder—and who could not thus become more and more identified with slavery and more and more ready to defend the institution?"

Actually, the fears of the slaveholders, reasonable as they might appear, were largely unjustified. Opposition to slavery was almost non-existent in the antebellum South. After all, non-slaveholders did not need to be instructed in the advantages of slavery to them. The evidence was all around them that the path to prestige as well as wealth lay through the acquisition of slaves and land. Moreover, in a society as socially competitive and mobile as that of the United States the denomination of blacks as biologically inferior served an important social function. Blacks were always below whites, regardless of the whites' achievements or lack thereof, thus putting a social floor beneath the status of all white people. In a society, in short, in which blacks were said to be inferior racially, it was most natural to justify slavery on the ground that blacks deserved to be slaves because of their race. In that way, then, the very social freedom and mobility that distinguished the United States as a land of opportunity for the poor lay, ironically, at the root of its peculiarly racial defense of slavery.

Perhaps the most striking irony of all concerning slavery in the history of the United States is that at the time the peculiar institution came under the most sustained and severe attack from outside the South, it was in law and in practice at its mildest. Eugene Genovese has noticed this tendency toward leniency in treatment and has contrasted it to the limitations on manumission that accompanied it. Historians, he writes, have correctly viewed the period from 1831 to 1861 "as one in which the treatment of slaves became progressively better. . . . The condition of the slaves worsened with respect to access to freedom and the promise of eventual emancipation; it got better with respect to material conditions of life." It should be noted that Genovese was referring to the law, for according to the census, the number of reported manumissions actually doubled between 1850 and 1860. During these years the laws prescribed adequate housing, food, clothing, and sometimes medical care for slaves. And as Kenneth Stampp has written, "by the 1850's, most of the codes had made cruelty a public offense even when not resulting in death." The point is not that these laws in themselves seriously altered the lot of the slave, but that the law reflected the changes that the earlier decision to close the slave trade had fostered.

Other changes in the law were not necessarily related to the need to maintain or augment the supply of slaves. Indeed, these legal alterations cannot be easily seen as a response to slave resistance or to the protection of bondage. I am referring to the safeguards that the law, both statutory and common, threw around the slave as a victim of crime and as a defendant. Before 1800 no southern state treated the killing of a slave as murder; by 1821 every state of the South did so. Penalties for breaking the law were usually lighter for whites than for blacks, but penalties were certainly exacted from whites for crimes against black slaves. Moreover, by the 1840s most of the states of the South had applied to slave criminals the common law crime of manslaughter and assault and battery rather than only murder for attacks upon whites. Furthermore, every slave state sought to protect slaves accused of capital crimes against biased juries by requiring legal counsel for the defendant slave. Several states undertook to pay for the lawyer when the master refused to do so. In both Arkansas and Missouri, slaves had a constitutional right to a court-appointed counsel in capital cases though free whites did not. In his study, Daniel Flanigan noted that not all appointed counsel were conscientious or diligent, but a surprising number of them were. Some were so dedicated that they followed up the case even after the slave was convicted. Both Alabama and Mississippi in the last two decades of the slave era developed a body of judicial interpretation that sought to protect the slave against the power of the master to extract or encourage confessions to crimes.

The growth of legal protections for slaves during the tense and recriminatory 1850s is not the only irony in the evolution of slavery. For whatever the motive behind this protection of the slave's rights as a human being, the result of it was further to entrench slavery. It is reasonable to suppose that the intention of the southern legislators and judges was to ameliorate the condition of the slave, to bring his condition closer to that recommended by

Christianity, and to offer the protections of the law to all persons, slave as well as free. Yet those protections served other purposes as well, as one Florida judge made evident when he wrote, "The crowning glory of our 'peculiar institutions' [is] that whenever life is involved, the slave stands upon as safe ground as the master." It was a way of justifying slavery not only to Christian southerners, but to those outside the South who sought to make a case against slavery by delineating its horrors and injustices. One Georgia judge predicted in 1851, soon after the legislature granted procedural equality to slaves, "this Act, as well as . . . numerous other provisions of the law" would show that Negroes were both property and "human creatures." The judge added, "For the justice and mercy of the slaveholding state of Georgia, an appeal well lies from the slanderous imputations of the ignorant, the fanatical, or the willfully base." It is probably true, too, that any improvement in the slave's condition as a result of the laws and practices played a part in making slave status less of a spur to discontent, flight, or revolt.

Until now, only ironies in the relationship between slavery and the values and development of American society have been identified. But there is another irony, the irony inherent in the way historians have treated the institution. At times the laudable effort to understand has resulted in distortion, and the drive to probe and compare has sometimes ended in half-truths.

After all that has been written in recent years about slavery, it is certainly a species of irony that not so long ago some historians were attempting to explain the meaning of America while failing to discuss slavery at all. Frederick Jackson Turner, for example, virtually ignored slavery in pointing to the frontier as the source of American nationality and democracy. Though he could describe in almost affectionate language the westward movement as the spread of democratic practice and ideas, he overlooked the role that same frontier played in giving a new lease on life to slavery, an institution that was the very antithesis of democracy and one that laid the foundation for the greatest failure of American political institutions—the secession of the South and the War for Southern Independence.

Turner's fellow Progressive historians, Charles and Mary Beard, were almost as blind as he was to the role of slavery in the making of American society. Nowhere in their massive *Rise of American Civilization* is there a description of the life of the slave or even what the slaves did. Indeed, it is clear that the Beards could not believe that the institution was central to an understanding of the last two decades of the antebellum period. Commenting on the coming of the Civil War, they wrote that "slavery is but one element, and if the number of abolitionists is any evidence, a minor element in the sweep of political and economic forces that occupied the attention of statesmen throughout the middle period and finally brought on the irrepressible conflict." Even the contradiction between the American creed and slavery did not strike them as real. When the Beards had finished describing the antislavery movement they were clearly baffled. "The sources of this remarkable movement are difficult to discover," they wrote. "Westermarck in two huge volumes devoted to the history of moral ideas, gives no clue to the inspiration of such a crusade."

Today slavery is no longer ignored in seeking to explain the nature of the American experience. Yet, among even the most recent writers about slavery, irony persists because they place so much emphasis upon the physical burden of slavery upon blacks. As Stanley Elkins correctly pointed out almost twenty years ago, the debate between Phillips and Stampp over the nature of slavery turned not only upon the racial beliefs of Phillips, but upon the weight of the burden of slavery on Negroes. That the issue continues to be important is shown by the reaction to Robert Fogel's and Stanley Engerman's recent *Time on the Cross*. At least one commentator denominated the book as pro-slavery, and when Columbia University awarded it the Bancroft Prize earlier this year, one of the trustees of that institution denounced the book for its alleged friendliness toward slavery. The vehemence with which *Time on the Cross* is attacked is not entirely related to its methodological weaknesses or errors of fact. It also stems from objections to its conclusions. My own reaction to *Time on the Cross* is severely critical. The book in my opinion is riddled with factual, interpretive, and methodological errors, unnecessary obscurantism, and excessive claims to novelty. I express this judgment here because I also believe that if the conclusions of *Time on the Cross* could have been sustained they would have been salutary for the study of slavery.

Among those conclusions, it will be remembered, was the assertion that slavery was not only considerably less onerous in practice than historians have said, but that the slaves contributed significantly to the prosperity of the antebellum economy of the South, not only by their labor, but by their managerial and other skills as well. The lot of the slave, Fogel and Engerman contended, was not much worse in conditions of life and work than that of free white workers in the North or South. Unfortunately, few elements in that general conclusion have been supported by the evidence in the book. Nonetheless, it is too bad that they have not been. If Fogel and Engerman had been able to establish their position, they would have registered a gain not only for cliometrics, but for an understanding of slavery as well. As they have pointed out, the very essence of bondage—the aspect that made it objectionable to abolitionists then, and to civilized society ever since—has been too often overlooked in recent writings on slavery.

The central objection to slavery is not that it was exploitative of the slave, or that it was disruptive of the slave family, or even that it was the cause of the slave's poor diet, inadequate housing, or high mortality, but that it was a denial of freedom. All the other aspects of slavery, many of which are certainly true historically, do not really get at more than the possible consequences of slavery; they are what logicians call "accidents." All historians, to be sure, must grapple at some time or other with the truth or falsity of any measurement of the "accidents" that may accompany slavery in different societies and times. But even if Fogel and Engerman had been able to show that—in regard to housing, health, diet, hours of work, and labor expended—the slave was on a par with the rural free man or woman of the South or the North, that conclusion would have neither justified slavery nor explained why blacks hated slavery or why some whites mounted a campaign to end it. The enormity of slavery lies in its denial of freedom.

The nature of the freedom that slavery denied is not a vague or abstract value. It can be spelled out quite specifically. At the very least slavery denied freedom of movement, as a result of which the slave could not choose his or her place to live, could not seek a spouse, visit others, travel, or simply wander. It also denied the opportunity to advance in occupational skills, in education, and usually in income. Slavery denied freedom of religious choice and of access to public information; it restricted choice of foods, housing, clothes, and use of time. It denied participation in government; it denied the right to refuse to work. Finally, all these denials were for life and were visited automatically upon the slave's children. The slave's range of choices were severely limited, no matter how kind, paternalistic, or generous the master was. These limitations on freedom occurred even if the caloric and nutritional content of the slave's diet, the square footage of his housing, and the quality of his clothing were in result on a par with those of free people. For even with those results choice had still been denied.

It is true that one can identify slaves who came close to exercising these freedoms. Such a case is Simon Gray, the Mississippi riverman who lived in his own house with his wife, commanded white boatmen, travelled without supervision from his master's plantation to New Orleans, and vacationed at the springs in Arkansas. Gray's range of freedoms was certainly greater than that enjoyed by many free Negroes and perhaps by many poor white people as well. Indeed, his very freedom measured the exceptional character of his personal status as a slave. We marvel at his status simply because the freedoms he enjoyed were not typical of slavery. Even so, the spectrum of freedoms he exercised was still not comparable to that of a free person. Gray could not change his job; he could not remain indefinitely in New Orleans or Arkansas; he could not provide for his children's future. And even those freedoms that he did exercise were always at the sufferance of another as a free person's comparable freedoms were not. Gray's unwonted range of freedom for a slave is the other side of the coin from that of free Negroes who petitioned to be returned to slavery. Their example reminds one that under certain circumstances freedom of choice might not be as valuable as a full stomach or personal and social security, just as Gray's condition is a reminder that slavery was a gamut of relationships, not a narrow, rigidly defined legal status. Both, however, are extremes. Only a minuscule number of free Negroes ever thought slavery was superior to freedom, though it is very likely that many of them lived under harsher physical and social circumstances than many slaves.

Ironically enough, the greater the emphasis placed upon the exploitative consequences of slavery, the farther one gets from a full understanding of the historical objections to slavery. At bottom, after all, it was not so much the barbarities or exploitation of slavery that aroused abolitionists against bondage as it was the overwhelming power of man over man. True, abolitionists in their determination to end slavery often emphasized the atrocities, as in Theodore Weld's famous tract of a thousand examples, *Slavery As It Is*. But even then the purpose was to show the consequences of inordinant power and to demonstrate the great injustice of slavery to those who were not convinced of the evil by an appeal to the right of all human beings to freedom. By emphasizing the physical oppression of slavery, one runs the risk of misunderstanding why slavery was abolished and why it deserved to be abolished. The oppression and physical deprivation had always been there; but, as David Brion Davis has shown, it was not until freedom became a central social value in western culture that slavery came under attack in any systematic way.

The emphasis upon the exploitative character of slavery threatens to distort an understanding of slavery in another way. Here, too, there is irony, because the intention of the historical interpreters has certainly been that of seeking understanding through a recognition of complexity. Yet what emerges from the interpretations is an emphasis upon what American slavery has in common with other forms of coercion at the expense of its unique aspect. Attention has been directed to the subordination inherent in slavery, thus relegating the racial element to the periphery.

It remains a fact that in the United States slavery was always a form of racial distinction. There was a time in antiquity when any one, regardless of nation, religion, or race, might be a slave. In the history of modern slavery, which began with the expansion of Europe in the sixteenth century, at no time and in no place were Europeans enslaved. Everywhere in the New World the slave was either an African or an Indian, that is, a person of color. It is surely significant that when Dr. Johnson complained about those who *"yelped"* about liberty yet were "drivers of negroes" he referred not to the legal status of the slaves but to their color. Johnson recognized what the laws of the slave states of the United States insisted upon—the status of slave and a dark skin always went together. No white person could legally be a slave in the United States nor were there any white slaves in Latin America.

This well-known fact has been minimized or simply assumed in some recent interpretations of American slavery, but with a consequent loss to a full understanding of the peculiar institution. The motivation behind the minimizing is understandable; it stems from a desire to move beyond glib and polemical appeals to racism in exploring the roots and nature of slavery. Laudable as the motives are and insightful as the resulting interpretations may be, playing down the role of race in the interpretation of slavery is to see the institution with only one eye. Edmund Morgan, for example, has emphasized the subordination aspect of slavery at the expense of race in an article entitled "Slavery and Freedom." In his article, Morgan sought to explain why slavery and freedom began together in early Virginia society. He certainly referred to the role of race in the enslavement of Negroes, but the burden of his argument was that class concerns were fundamental.

Richard Wade is yet another historian who, though aware of the racial component of slavery, seems to end up emphasizing what slavery had in common with other forms of subordination. Unlike Morgan, Wade did not consciously emphasize the subordination in slavery in his work *Slavery in the Cities*. Indeed, he often referred to bondage as a racial institution. Yet his analysis emphasized slavery as a form of oppression rather than as a form of racial distinction. He concluded that there was an inherent conflict between urban life and slavery, citing as evidence the undeniable decline in the proportion of slaves in the cities of the South between 1820 and 1860.

Cliometrician Claudia Goldin has mounted an elaborate statistical argument against Wade's conclusion, but her evidence does not seem as convincing as the evidence from the comparative history of slavery in cities. In both Peru and Brazil, in regard to which there is recent information, there appeared to be no such apparent conflict between urban life and slavery. In fact, slavery flourished in Lima and in Rio de Janeiro, in the latter city right down into the last quarter of the nineteenth century. It is true that Charleston and New Orleans were not Rio or Lima, but that is precisely the point. All four are cities and it was urban life in general that Wade envisioned as the threat to slavery. In the light of the slave experience in Rio and Lima, it seems it was not the city as such that threatened slavery in the American South—if it was threatened at all—but the attitudes of whites toward slaves who were black. In respect to attitudes toward colored people the cities of the American South differed considerably from the cities of Latin America. In short, in accounting for what he interpreted as a weakening of slavery in southern cities, Wade seems to have overlooked the race of the slaves while concentrating upon their status. In determining why slavery seemed to be declining in the cities, it might be better to look to the fears of whites about blacks, than to the worries of slaveholders about their subordinates.

More recently, David Brion Davis, in the second volume of his history of anti-slavery, also emphasized the subordination evident in slavery while playing down the race of the slaves. In all kinds of analysis, to be sure, the historian must often ignore one aspect of a subject while emphasizing another. But more than that seems to be involved here, for at the close of his volume Davis omitted the fact of race altogether. On his last page, in discussing slavery as a species of subordination, he wrote: "Slavery itself has the great virtue, as an ideal model, of being clear-cut. Yet the model is so clear-cut that both abolitionists and later historians often obscured the complexities of actual bondage. . . . Furthermore, as I have tried to suggest in this study, the model was so clear-cut that it tended to set slavery off from other species of barbarity and oppression—except when an apologist said, in effect, why should Negro slaves complain when pauper children are starving and sailors are lashed every day?"

Eugene Genovese, too, tends to combine the status of the slave with the status of the worker in general, even though in his book *Roll, Jordan, Roll* he was at pains to trace the origins of modern black nationalism back to the life of the antebellum slave. He wrote on his opening page: "By definition and in essence [slavery] was a system of class rule, in which some people lived off the labor of others. American slavery subordinated one race to another and thereby rendered its fundamental class relationships more complex and ambiguous; but they remained class relationships." Indeed, in pondering the many subtle psychological analyses in his book, I was struck again and again by the similarity between the relationship of master and slave as Genovese depicted it and the relationship between free worker and employer. On the last page, the matter of slave consciousness itself was put in class terms. "But even the preachers, drivers, and mechanics," Genovese wrote, "could not decisively organize their people politically, and therefore, could not move them toward explicit class consciousness. They did, however, contribute toward the formulation of a protonational consciousness, expressed primarily through religious sensibility that enabled a mass of oppressed individuals to cohere as a people." Yet, one wonders, where is the influence of color or race in Genovese's analysis? Was the "class" character of slavery the force that welded the many different African nations that came to the New World into the single category of "Negroes"? Or was it more likely the whites' insistence upon racial distinction that indiscriminately blended them into the single category of "colored"? Moreover, slavery had this homogenizing effect only in the United States. In every other slave society in the New World, a clear and important social distinction was made between free blacks and free mulattoes, that is, between people of different skin color or appearance. In one instance (the United States), distinctions of color were ignored while in the other (Latin America) they were asserted. Color, not class, is today the basis of distinctions between former slaves and white people, as it was earlier between slaves and free people. Slavery was undoubtedly a species of subordination, but more importantly it was a form of racial distinction and oppression.

An emphasis upon slavery as a form of class also obscures the psychological and social import of the fact that only blacks were slaves. Certainly blacks and whites knew of, and responded to, that visual fact. That only blacks were slaves could not help but affect blacks' perception of each other or blacks' and whites' perceptions of themselves, as the many quotations referring to color in *Roll, Jordan, Roll* make plain. Class status also affects social perception, but it always lacks the powerful and visual element of color or race.

Finally, by emphasizing the class character of slavery, one is in danger of misunderstanding the social attitudes of whites toward manumission and toward free Negroes in the antebellum South. Professor Genovese has observed that, as the physical treatment of the slaves improved in the course of the last decades of the antebellum period, the legal opportunities for manumission diminished. In calling attention to these contrary developments, Genovese further observed that often the same white men were active in the two movements. "Their position made perfect sense," he concluded. "Make the South safe for slaveholders by confirming the blacks in perpetual slavery and by making it possible for them to accept their fate," that is, to be slaves forever. I find such logic unclear. Why should slaveholders pass laws prohibiting themselves from freeing their own slaves? Who threatened to compel them to free their slaves against their will? After all, the laws restricting manumission were not laws against abolitionists, they were laws limiting a man's right over his human property. There does not seem to be any "class" reason from the standpoint of the slaveholders for the laws against manumission. Indeed, on the surface, the existence of such laws seems to suggest that there was a danger that some slaveholders might want to free their slaves.

Moreover, after noting conditions in Latin America it is evident that opposition to manumission was not considered necessary from the standpoint of a slaveholder as simply an owner of labor. Limitations on manumission were functional only in a society that feared free black people. Manumission was easy throughout Latin America, as Genovese and others have pointed out many times, for free blacks did not threaten that social order. In the United States, however, free blacks did threaten the social order; free blacks threatened the tranquillity of *all* white people, not just slaveholders. The passage of these laws against manumission was dictated, not by the need to preserve slavery as a system of class relations, but by the desire to keep down the number of free blacks. It was the fact that slaves were black that made the whites determined not to make manumission easy.

When one recognizes this social fact, then it is easy to understand a point made by Ira Berlin in his recent sensitive study of free Negroes in the South. Berlin noted that as the antebellum years wore on, the restrictions against free Negroes increased and hardened. The laws tightening manumission and those forcing free Negroes into slavery were really two sides of the same shield. Both were ways of keeping blacks under control, for in the minds of most white southerners the best method for controlling blacks was slavery. The peculiar institution was *Negro* slavery, not just bondage or subordination in general. To understand American slavery it is necessary to move beyond Hegel and his conception of lordship and bondage; it is necessary to recognize that modern slavery was first of all a relationship between whites and blacks. It is necessary to recognize, also, that racial consciousness and antagonism have been as basic and as functional in human affairs as class consciousness and antagonism.

Race was not the only element that differentiated slavery from other forms of oppression. Conceptually and practically, slavery was different because the master of slaves could call upon the power of the state in designating his subordinated workers as a piece of property. The paradox of seeing human beings as property was certainly a source of problems, but it surely made the power of the master of slaves greater than that of any other master. It is quite true that the master of slaves might not have chosen to exercise that power, so that in practice a slave might actually have been better off than a free person. David Brion Davis points out, for example, that antislavery people in England distinguished between slaves and those so-called free workers who lived on the edge of starvation and were even compelled to wear collars.

Although Davis implies that the distinction drawn by the abolitionists was illusory, I would like to argue that the distinction was not as metaphysical as he seems to suggest. In certain extreme cases, to be sure, freedom of choice might be an illusion, especially if one were near starvation and compelled to wear a collar or some other sign of an especially degraded status. The illusion would be complete when that situation was contrasted with a slave's absence of choice when his food, clothing, and housing were assured and he was spared outward signs of degradation. But we are concerned with central tendencies of institutions here, not extreme cases. To dwell upon the continuum between class and slavery is to overlook the historical, not to say the legal, discontinuity between slavery and freedom. For even if one can in theory show a spectrum of subordination running from complete freedom to abject slavery, in historical fact as in law the difference was plain. As Moses Finley has pointed out, "what separates the slave from the rest, including the serf or peon, is the totality of his powerlessness in principle, and for that the idea of property is juristically the key—hence the term 'chattel slave.'" The difference is best demonstrated by emphasizing the loss of freedom under slavery, not by pointing to the brutality or exploitation that slavery had in common with other forms of subordination. For as Professor Davis had shown in his most recent book, it was the denial of freedom that evoked the opposition which finally extirpated slavery from western culture.

At the same time, while emphasizing the denial of freedom that lay at the heart of the institution, we must not ignore or overlook slavery's other role—as a form of distinction between peoples of different color. For in our effort to understand the complexities of slavery it would be the saddest of ironies if we should forget that the institution was not just American slavery, but American *Negro* slavery.

Slavery—The World's Burden

EUGENE D. GENOVESE

Americans long viewed slavery, the terrible war it precipitated, and the painful legacy it left southerners and northerners, whites and blacks, as peculiar national problems. In recent decades, however, our vision has broadened to place slavery and especially race relations in a hemispheric perspective. At the grave risk of attempting much too much, I should like to address the legacy of slavery in still a larger perspective. In defense, I would remind critics that no one any longer doubts that an advanced state of economic integration and international power struggle marked the world of the nineteenth century. Nor does anyone doubt the momentous impact of European industralism, nationalism, liberalism, democracy, and imperialism on the world at large. But then it becomes necessary to step back from national and regional peculiarities and to explore the links between these forces in the United States and those in the countries with which the United States was increasingly interacting in the world economy and in world politics.

From this point of view, I propose to assess, however tentatively, the role of American slaveholders as well as of Europe's great landholding classes in the shaping of the world in which we now live. Simultaneously, I shall attempt to assess the role of the slaves in the shaping of the resistance movements of modern times and of the rise of new and revolutionary collectivist societies.

Slavery burdened not merely the United States but the entire world with the creation of powerful landholding classes based on unfree labor. These classes enormously strengthened opposition to the revolutionary tidal wave of bourgeois liberalism and democracy, although slavery had reemerged in the modern world largely under bourgeois auspices. The spread of capitalism in Europe had created a mass market for cotton, sugar, tobacco, and other plantation staples. The growth of a capitalist shipping industry had made possible the magnitude of the slave trade, and other capitalist sectors had provided not only the capital but the commodities necessary to sustain the African connection and service the American plantations. Plantation slavery arose in the Americas as part of the process of international capitalist development.

The specific conditions of plantation life and organization, however, provided fertile ground for the emergence of retrograde ruling classes. And for the moment it makes little difference whether those new landed classes are viewed as variant capitalist classes, as incipient new aristocracies, or as some kind of hybrid. Clearly, they began by advancing world economic development and ended by threatening to stifle it. Initially, these ruling classes brought millions of Africans and other self-sufficient peoples into commodity production for a world market, provided commodities needed to sustain capitalist expansion in Europe, created new markets for burgeoning European industry, and accumulated capital, some of which spurred European industry directly and more of which indirectly contributed to market formation and commercial expansion.

In the end, however, they built no technologically advanced, economically progressive, politically and militarily self-reliant nations of their own; much less did they create anything their warmest admirers could recognize as a great culture or civilization. The very forces of initial dynamism had become frozen in place. In one country after another sad decline followed stagnation, at least relative to the progressive capitalist sectors of the world; retrogression followed an orgy of prosperity. The West Indies became cultural as well as economic wrecks; Brazil lost its chance to become a great power; and the American South became this country's least dynamic and prosperous major region—to put it charitably. The great slaveholding countries moved from a central position in the worldwide advance of capitalism, with its unprecedented standards of living even for the masses, to a periphery of misery, poverty, discouragement, and general embarrassment. But, of course, for the slaves whose blood and toil had created the original wealth, those countries had never been anything else.

The underdevelopment and backwardness that still grip most of the old slaveholding countries have provided burden enough for today's world to bear. But much more remains at stake. The slaveholders of the Americas in effect reinforced the political role of the declining landholding classes of Europe, first in opposing the spread of bourgeois liberalism and then, after their own defeat by the bourgeoisie, in opposing the spread of democracy. The influence of the slaveholders and the European landed classes was uniformly reactionary, although by no means uniform in specific content or intensity. In Europe, in Latin America, and, to a lesser extent, even in the United States, these classes significantly retarded the great movements for recognition of autonomy of the individual and the legitimate participation of the masses in political life.

The intervention of these landed classes on the side of reaction came at a fateful moment in the history of Europe and America—at the very moment at which the bourgeoisie itself, faced with threats from the Left, was being forced to recognize the contradiction between its historic commitment to individual freedom and its early, if always uneasy, flirtation with democracy and equality. Jacobinism, after all, was quintessentially a bourgeois movement. By the middle of the nineteenth century, however, any form of Jacobinism looked like socialism, communism, or anarchy to a bourgeoisie increasingly disillusioned with mass politics.

Even the most liberal bourgeoisies—those of England, France, and the United States—which continued to adhere to some form of democratic commitment, turned outward in an attempt to solve the social question at home at the expense of colonial peoples. The legacy of the old colonialism and its ideologically essential racism served their strategy well, as did the remnants of the old landed classes directly. One need not follow Joseph Schumpeter in attributing modern imperialism to the atavistic tendencies of the old landholding elites to recognize the importance of their role.

Disputes continue to rage over the character and class cohesion of the slaveholders of the Old South and of other countries as well. These disputes may never be settled. Some things, however, are beyond dispute even among historians, who rarely agree on anything. Quarrels may arise over the extent to which the slaveholders felt guilt about owning slaves, but no one doubts that as a group, guilt and misgivings or no, they were determined to defend their property and power. In this respect in 1861 they stood alongside the slaveholding planters of Brazil and Cuba, alongside the Russian lords—elegantly delineated by Turgenev, Dostoevski, and Tolstoi and unforgetably satirized by Gogol—lords who, with the support of such brutal rulers as Catherine the Great, had slowly reduced their serfs to a status approaching that of slaves, and who set a high standard of pitiless brutality in the suppression of peasant revolts. And as late as 1861 the southern slaveholders also stood alongside such dying but still deadly landholding classes as those of Poland, Hungary, Italy, and Japan, which commanded unfree or only technically free labor in regimes even then looked upon as barbarous by both the bourgeois and laboring classes of Western Europe.

Historical analogies and parallels are always dangerous; their uses rest in being suggestive rather than in being elements in some equation. The southern slaveholders were not transplanted boyars or Junkers or Polish lords or even Brazilian *senhores de engenho*. Each of these classes had its own traditions, sensibilities, characteristics, notions of civilized life, and peculiar relationship to labor; each had its own internal divisions. The slaveholders of Virginia were not quite the same as those of Louisiana, any more than the *senhores de engenho* of the sugar-growing Brazilian Northeast were quite the same as the *fazendeiros* of the coffee-growing Brazilian South. And yet, they did, in a broad sense, represent variations on one side of a great historical divide.

These classes—however defined by historians as rural capitalists, aristocrats, prebourgeois landlords, or whatever—represented, in different degrees, stubborn opposition to the emerging forces of the modern world. Some of them were remnants of a world steadily being overthrown by the expansion of world capitalism. Others, including the American slaveholders, had their class origins in that very expansion. But all, to the extent that they could create and consolidate their political power, had increasing difficulty in living in a world of emerging cities, industries, mechanization, international finance, and the participation of the masses in politics.

From an economic point of view, these landed classes commanded regimes that, however profitable in the narrow sense, lacked the developmental possibilities of regimes based on free labor and, therefore, the military possibilities for survival in a world of increasingly competitive nation-states. The Junkers learned that hard lesson during the Napoleonic wars, although not until Bismarck's time did they learn it well enough. The Russian lords learned it, to the extent that they learned it at all, during the Crimean War and the peasant rebellions that came before and after. The Brazilians had their own national disaster during the Paraguayan War and the unravelling of their social and political structure. And the Japanese suffered the humiliation of the so-called opening by the West. The nineteenth century, in short, demonstrated from one end of the world to the other that the path of safety and survival for old ruling classes as well as for new nations was the path of accommodation to the irresistible advance of nationalism and industrial capitalism. Whether in a death struggle or a reluctant compromise, the great landholders who survived as individuals, as families, or as whole classes did so at the price of surrendering their traditional ways of life as well as their political autonomy, not merely to new men but to a new class based on the property relations of money and markets.

The passing of the great landed classes—however slow, partial, or disguised—marked the final victory and consolidation of a worldwide system of capitalist production and, with it, of a new world view or, rather, a new complex of antagonistic world views. In a sense, the economic struggle between contending economic systems had long ago been settled. The decisive struggles had become political, ideological, and moral. That is, from the sixteenth century onward, the new system of capitalist production developing in Northwestern Europe was spreading across the world. This new system embraced something much more important, something more decisive, than international commerce. International commerce had played an important role in the ancient world and in the great empires of China and India. And it was particularly notable in the magnificent expansion of Islam across the Mediterranean basin into Spain and black Africa and eastward to China, Central Asia, and Indonesia. Without a vigorous and well-organized commercial system the great Muslim caliphates of the eighth and ninth centuries and beyond, with their brilliant contributions to art, science, philosophy, and law, would have been impossible. Yet none of these commercially developed civilizations succeeded in creating an integrated worldwide system of production and exchange; nor did they even try.

The spread of capitalism in early modern Europe, therefore, marked the rise of a new mode of production—that is, of new social relations based on personal freedom and on a revolutionary and apparently self-revolutionizing technology associated with those relations. And it also marked a revolution in human values, the decisive feature of which was precisely the freedom of labor—that is, the transformation of labor-power into a commodity. That freedom liberated human beings to work for themselves and to accumulate wealth; it also forced the laboring poor out of their traditional dependence on the protection, such as it was, of lords and patrons and placed them under the stern whip of marketplace necessity.

This new mode of production gave rise to a new theory of property. The right of the individual to property both in his own person and his labor-power constituted not merely its economic but its moral foundation. And once that theory of property took root, the very definition of the rights and duties of the individual in relation to the state changed dramatically, as did the content of race relations.

True, the Christian tradition had long established the principle of equality before God and the responsibility of the individual for his actions. The Christian ethic had long stressed that, while men must render unto Caesar the things that are Caesar's, men must also assume full responsibility for rendering unto God the things that are God's; and God's things included the moral sanctity of individual life and the immortality of the soul. But this great tradition, itself so revolutionary and heroic, did not destroy the principle of property in man, and the specific history of the Catholic Church had actually reinforced and legitimized the principle of class subordination. It is in this sense that David Brion Davis, in his excellent book *The Problem of Slavery in the Age of Revolution*, refers to the new bourgeois idea of freedom, especially in its Hegelian form, as bearing only superficial resemblance to the Christian idea, although the early emergence of the Christian idea of freedom in Western Civilization decisively prepared the ground for the emergence of the secular bourgeois idea during the Enlightenment.

The spread of capitalism revolutionized thought as well as material life. Liberalism, in those eighteenth- and nineteenth-century forms which today are usually associated with free-market conservatives, became the dominant ideology of the bourgeoisie. This new ruling class took its stand on the freedom of the individual and on some form of political representation. In time new bourgeois nation-states, most notably Germany and Japan, would assume a more authoritarian political stance. But even there, industrial capitalism carried with it an expanded commitment to individual freedom and even to broadened political participation.

In short, the forward movement of capitalist relations of production required a new definition of the rights and responsibilities of the individual and, as John C. Calhoun, George Fitzhugh, and other leading southerners understood, posed a powerful challenge to all previous ideas of an organic society within which some men assumed major responsibility for the lives and well-being of others. The issue between the bourgeoisie and the older landed classes, therefore, inexorably became the moral question of the nature and destiny of human life. For centuries political leaders deliberately obscured this issue and arranged compromises to deal with its manifestations. In the end, however, two irreconcilable world views met in combat, sometimes quickly or peacefully resolved and sometimes, as in the United States, resolved by a brutal test of physical strength.

But this struggle was not to be so cleancut, if only because the wonderful new freedom bestowed on the laboring classes carried with it a good dose of hunger, neglect, deprivation, misery, and death. The roots of the working-class democratic and socialist movement lay in the attempt of artisans and craftsmen to resist the destruction of their independent way of life and their absorption into the marketplace of labor. But by the middle of the nineteenth century, the struggle of the artisans and craftsmen had irrevocably been lost; its impulses and ideas of equality, fraternity, and democracy had passed into the working-class movement, most militantly into its socialist contingent.

Accordingly, the old landed classes faced ideological and political challenge both from bourgeois liberalism and from a proletarian socialism with origins in bourgeois thought but increasingly independent of it. Recall, therefore, the dire warnings of Calhoun,

James Hammond, Fitzhugh, G. F. Holmes, Henry Hughes, and others that the bourgeoisie would rue the day it destroyed the landed classes and with them, a great bulwark against lower-class radicalism. And, in fact, in many countries the bourgeoisies did unite with their old landowning enemies to turn back the challenge from the Left. Still, in this unequal partnership, the bourgeoisie steadily strengthened its position as senior partner, and the landowners steadily surrendered their old way of life to become, in effect, a mere appendage of the capitalist class. The old organic relations among men disappeared, sometimes quickly, sometimes slowly as in the more patriarchal areas of the New South in which paternalism lingered well into the twentieth century, if only as an echo of a bygone era.

But, even in such countries as Germany, Japan, and Italy, the upper-class coalition agreed upon the essential bourgeois principles of freedom of labor, at least in the marketplace sense, while it took a hard line against the democratic and egalitarian impulses that had themselves arisen within the earlier bourgeois revolutions.

Thus, even the most admirable and genuinely paternalistic of the old landed classes generally surrendered the best of their own traditions—the organic view of society and the idea that men were responsible for each other—while they retained the worst of their traditions—their general class and race arrogance and particular contempt for the laboring classes and darker races. These vices they offered as a gift to a triumphant bourgeoisie, which had acquired enough of the same already. The postbellum South provided a striking, if qualified, example of this worldwide reactionary tendency. The Calhouns and Fitzhughs might have been startled to learn that the great conservative coalition they had called for could come into being only after the destruction of their beloved plantation-slave regime. But it could not have been otherwise; nor, despite appearances, was it otherwise in Germany or Japan. In every case the terms of the coalition had to include, as

36   Slavery—The World's Burden

sine qua non, acceptance of the bourgeois principle of property relations and the hegemony of the marketplace, no matter how qualified by authoritarianism and state regulation of the economy. In the United States the price was relatively cheap—the postbellum South suffered political reaction and economic stagnation; the nation as a whole suffered from the strengthening of the conservative elements in its political life. But, on balance, the United States, more than any other country with the possible exception of England, successfully blended the classic bourgeois commitment to individual freedom with the more radical currents of democracy and mass participation in politics, and, in addition, provided a high standard of material comfort.

In presenting the southern slaveholders as one of many landed classes arrayed against the progressive currents of the eighteenth and especially nineteenth centuries, I intend no identity or equation. As a class, the southern slaveholders had their own extraordinary virtues as well as vices and could not escape being American in their inheritance of traditions of freedom and democracy; indeed, with justice they claimed to have helped shape those traditions. The constitutions of states like Mississippi ranked among the country's most democratic, and South Carolina's conservatism made it an exception among the slave states. The slave states maintained a degree of freedom of speech, assembly, and the press that might have been the envy of the people of much of Europe, a degree of freedom unheard of in the rest of the world. Even most of the poorer white men had some access to politics and some effect on the formation of social policy. And if the white literacy rate and general educational standard opened the South to just abolitionist criticism, they still compared favorably with those of most other countries.

Hence, many learned and able historians have stressed the "Americanness" of the Old South and viewed its deviations from national norms as a mere regional variation on a common theme. And let it be conceded that by many useful criteria even the most reactionary elements of the slaveholding class had more in common with northern Americans of all classes than with the Russian boyars or Prussian Junkers.

The great difficulty with this interpretation, however, is that it loses sight of slavery's overwhelming impact on the South, of the dangerous political role it was playing in American national life, and of the fundamental historical tendency it represented. If world-historical processes of the nineteenth century are viewed as a coherent whole, then that cranky and sometimes insincere reactionary George Fitzhugh was right in seeing the slaveholding South as part of a great international counterrevolutionary movement against the spread of a bourgeois world order. The great problem for the most progressive, liberal, and democratically inclined slaveholders and other proslavery southerners was that the slavery question could not be isolated as a regional peculiarity occasioned by a special problem of racial adjustment.

Consider the basic question of political freedom. Foreign travelers often supported southern claims to being a liberal-spirited and tolerant people. What northern state, for example, was sending Jews to the United States Senate? The only drawback concerned abolitionist propaganda that threatened to unleash anarchy and bloodshed. And here, southern intolerance was neither paranoid nor irrational nor blindly neanderthal; it represented a local version of the elementary principle of self-preservation. And here, the slaves themselves ruined their masters. No matter that they rose in insurrection rarely and in small numbers. As the medieval scholastics insisted, existence proves possibility. However infrequent and militarily weak the appearance of a Gabriel Prosser, a Denmark Vesey, or a Nat Turner, they and others like them did exist, and so, therefore, did the danger of slave revolt. White southerners would have been mad to teach significant numbers of their slaves to read and write, to permit abolitionist literature to fall into their hands, to take an easy view of politicians, clergymen, and editors who so much as questioned the morality and justice of the very foundation of their social order and domestic peace. Many historians would go further and argue that the economic, social, and political consequences of slavery ill served the mass of whites too, and that agitation of the slavery question threatened to open a class struggle among whites. I agree with that view, but, if valid, it merely provides a case of over-determination.

On national terrain, slave-state politicians fought for the gag rule and thereby threatened the sacred right of petition. They had to advocate tampering with the mails, had to defend a measure of lynch law against people who talked too much, had to proclaim boldly that a free press could not safely be allowed to be too free, and had to offend northern sensibilities by demanding a fugitive slave law that bluntly doubted the scrupulousness of the vaunted jury system. The slaveholders demonstrated time and time again that, despite their honest protestations of respect for freedom and even democracy, the exigencies of their social system were drag-ging them irresistibly toward political and social policies flagrantly tyrannical, illiberal, and undemocratic, at least by American stan-dards. No matter how much and how genuinely they tried to stand by their cherished Jeffersonian traditions, they were compelled, step-by-step, down the road charted by their most extreme theorists, for their commitment to survival as a ruling class as well as a master race left them less and less choice.

It was not necessary for the slaveholders and their supporters to embrace Fitzhugh's extreme doctrines; indeed, it is doubtful that they ever could or would have. Yet, the thoughtful Calhoun tried to reform the federal Constitution to make it safe for slavery, and younger politicians during the 1850s made desperate attempts to bully northern consent to increasingly unpalatable measures. From a northern perspective, slaveholding southerners, drunk with their near absolute power over human beings, had become tyrannical, intransigent, and incapable of reasoned compromise. From a southern perspective, even friendly and moderate northerners were willing to acquiesce in measures that would threaten southern property and social order and, to make matters worse, were increasingly willing to view slavery as a kind of moral leprosy. Both sides were right in their own terms, for slavery had, as Tocqueville and others warned, separated two great white American peoples even more deeply in moral perspective than in material interest. And moral separation, quite as readily as material, threatened confrontation and war once made manifest on political terrain.

We end then with the paradox that the southern slaveholders, who might have been qualified among the world's most liberal and even democratic ruling classes, qualified in the eyes of their northern fellow Americans as a grossly reactionary and undemocratic force—much as the hardened and retrograde landowners of Europe so qualified in the eyes of the liberal bourgeoisie. The southern slaveholders were doing in American terms what the English colonial slaveholders were doing when they threw their weight against parliamentary reform, what the French slaveholders in the colonies and the aristocrats at home were doing when they supported the counterrevolution, what the Prussian Junkers were doing when they demolished the liberal movement of 1848, and what the Russian boyars were doing when they suicidally refused to limit the imperial power.

Some would argue—and they may well be right—that the greatest burden inherent in the legacy of slavery has been the division and hostility engendered among the races of the world. But few if any would seriously doubt that white Europe's enslavement of darker peoples and eventual conquest of the world had, as primary object, enrichment and economic exploitation. That racial antipathies predated colonialism and slavery presents fascinating and important complications of enduring significance; it does not, however, refute the basic proposition. Moreover, centuries of slavery and racial rationale laid the indispensable ideological basis for the new colonialism and imperialism of the late nineteenth century. Africa directly and Asia indirectly were, after all, divided among the big powers after slavery had been abolished. In today's era of decolonization and a new balance of power, the bitterness attendant upon a long history of oppression, degradation, uneven material development, and racism has risen to haunt us. So obvious is this feature of the burden of our past that little elaboration would seem necessary. Accordingly, I shall restrict myself to one point—the historical necessity of the racial basis of modern slavery.

It is at best a dangerous half-truth to attribute the cruelties of slavery to white racism, however much racism contributed to the specific cruelties of plantation life. The Germans, Russians, Hungarians, and other white European landowners traditionally dealt with their serfs and peasants no less cruelly and often more so. From France to Russia the great lords even pretended that their serfs somehow derived from different racial or ethnic stock and constituted subject peoples apart. Yet, slavery arose in the New World at the very moment, and under the same impulses, as the spread of the bourgeois idea of property and its attendant respect for the autonomy of the individual. Even the traditional, seignorial, Catholic countries could not prevent the spread of such ideas, however much they slowed their progress. Modern slavery therefore, tended toward exclusion of its victims from the community of man. Not only or primarily did this tendency define slaves as things; rather, even when it accepted, as it had to, the humanity of the slaves, it had to assign that very humanity to a lower level of moral being. In no other way could slavery be reconciled with the advancing bourgeois ethos. Thus, slavery in a bourgeois world context required a violent racism not merely as an ideological rationale but as a psychological imperative. The effects of this psychology, as well as ideology, were to be reinforced by postslavery imperialism and now threaten a worldwide disaster. With due respect to Chairman Mao's theory of cultural revolution, but also with much skepticism, I submit that historical experience leads to the conclusion that it is immeasurably easier to overthrow not only governments but social systems than it is to alter men's souls.

The tough old landed classes of Europe, in short, received fresh support from the new landed classes thrown up by plantation slavery in the Americas. Even after their defeats, they did not disappear but were absorbed to reinforce the most reactionary and antidemocratic tendencies within the capitalist classes. As the European bourgeoisie faced challenge from the socialist Left, it retreated in varying degrees from the dream of a reconciliation of individual freedom with mass democracy. But what of the other side of this historical process? The slaves, in their resistance to slavery, prepared the way for the struggle of future laboring classes against the bourgeoisie. When the ex-slaves entered capitalist society as free men, they played a role reverse of that of their former masters. Through no fault of their own, however, the contribution of the slaves to the revolutionary and radical movements of subsequent generations also has had tragic and increasingly ominous consequences. In this respect, too, ex-masters and ex-slaves proved incapable of separating themselves completely from each other.

To begin at the end, with emancipation considered in an international political framework . . . the political history of emancipation consisted of a series of nationally discrete but interlocking movements, which, taken together, formed a single process. It began with the French Revolution, gathered strength with the movement to abolish the slave trade, had its turning point with the great British Emancipation Act of 1833, climaxed with a bloody, fratricidal war in the United States, and ended with the ostensibly peaceful but, in its own less dramatic and less extensive way, violent enough abolition in Brazil. The first emancipation did not arise from the parliamentary niceties in London, but from the conjuncture of the Jacobin ascendancy in revolutionary Paris with the greatest slave revolt in world history in Saint-Domingue. True, when the counter-revolution triumphed in France, Napoleon reinstituted slavery in the French islands. But even that great if brutal man could not impose his will on the richest and most important of the islands—St.-Domingue—for the simple reason that the blacks successfully transformed their revolt into a national revolution and manifested enough power to sustain it.

The revolution in St.-Domingue, rechristened Haiti, marked a watershed, not only in the history of slavery but in world history. One-half to two-thirds of the blacks there had been born in Africa and, in a contemporary phrase, did "not speak two words of French." Yet, at the peak of their political movement, Toussaint L'Ouverture, the revolution's leader of genius, issued a constitution that proclaimed these ex-slaves to be "free and French." That expression signified a great deal more than a political device designed to give the new black state full autonomy and freedom under the protection of and in alliance with a strong European power. And it emphatically did not imply a wish to transform black Afro-Americans into white Europeans. It signified the common and plausible identification of the cause of freedom, equality, and fraternity with the hegemony of the French nation in its world-shaking revolution. Further reflection on the meaning of the Haitian revolution—sometimes suggestively called by friend and foe alike, "The French Revolution in St.-Domingue"—provides a serviceable way to explore the larger significance of the rise and fall of the slaveholding classes in the Americas, particularly in the Old South.

What was St.-Domingue before the revolution? What was Haiti afterwards? In 1789 a small class of whites lived off the brutally exploited labor of a half-million blacks. In St.-Domingue there was the complication of a solidly entrenched class of mulatto slaveholders, many of them extremely wealthy, who also lived off the labor of black slaves; but this complication may be set aside, despite its critical importance during the political and military course of the revolution. An intermediary class of lowerclass and petty-bourgeois whites—the so-called *petits blancs*—filled out a brittle social structure and contributed, as best they could, to making the life of the slaves as miserable as possible.

Without playing relativity games, it is safe to say that few slaves in Mississippi, however oppressed they had reason to feel, would have wanted to change places with the slaves who labored under the Draconian regime in St.-Domingue. Whereas the slaves in Mississippi and the Old South lived with a degree of material comfort and community stability adequate to reproduce themselves, the slaves of St.-Domingue lived under conditions unfavorable to reproduction, so that the economy required the steady importation of Africans. And on the strength of that grisly regime of class exploitation and racial oppression, St.-Domingue emerged as the world's single richest, most profitable, most coveted colony.

The whites who commanded that blood-money fell roughly into two groups—the big planters and the *petits blancs*. The intermediary strata of small slaveholders, businessmen, and others did not have the numbers or potential power of the yeomanry of the Old South and may also be ignored in this overview. The white planters came from all classes—decadent French aristocrats trying to recoup lost fortunes in an increasingly capitalist world, French and other European bourgeois-on-the-rise trying to make a killing in the islands so as to live like gentlemen in Bordeaux or Paris, and desperate men from the lower orders who sought to climb the economic and social ladder over the broken bodies of fellow human beings. These diverse groups together aspired, despite generally seedy origins, to substitute for the older European aristocracy, then in headlong economic decline. And like most converts, they were often "more Catholic than the Pope" in their commitment to hierarchy, order imposed from above, and a repressive policy toward those lower-class and middle-class individuals who entertained ridiculous ideas of equality and personal freedom. They represented, a vigorous, new, wealthy, and dangerous reserve army for French and European reaction. During the

French Revolution and its aftermath they stood for the counter-revolution of big landed property against both the democratic program of the Jacobins and the rural egalitarianism of the peasant risings. Symbolically, Josephine, Napoleon's first wife and a power in her own right, was a colonial. Through the struggles for liberalization and democratization that racked France in the uprisings of 1830, 1848, and 1871, the survivors of the *ancien regime* landowning classes, including the remnants of the old colonial slavetrading and slaveowning elites, fought to hold back the rising tide of bourgeois values, whether in the liberal form of parliamentarism, free-labor, and individual liberty or in the neo-Jacobin and emerging socialist form of equality and the redistribution of property.

And what of the slaves of St.-Domingue, now citizens of Haiti, free, although not as Toussaint had hoped "free and French"? Conventional wisdom tells us that they exchanged white for black and mulatto masters, that Toussaint himself and, after him, Jean Dessalines and Henri Christophe imposed a harsh regime of quasi-forced labor, that the economy never did recover, and that Haiti stands today as the hemisphere's most wretched poverty-stricken country. This conventional wisdom, as usual, contains an undeniable measure of truth; and, also as usual, it adds up to a gross distortion.

I shall risk here all the dangers attendant upon the briefest summary of the complex history of the Haitian revolution and counterrevolution. Toussaint and his immediate successors imposed a regime of strict labor discipline—they sent the ex-slaves back to the plantations and dealt out severe punishments to those who refused to work. Toussaint aimed to restore sugar production and to rebuild the export sector. He understood, despite his being a middle-aged, barely literate, generally uneducated, recently self-liberated slave, that the new black nation would recede into poverty and cultural barbarism unless it could build elementary industry, schools, churches, cultural institutions, and all the accoutrements of a civilized modern state. He knew that nothing would be possible in isolation and that a firm political and military alliance with revolutionary France was essential to national survival. Toussaint knew that economic and cultural reconstruction, as well as the support of a European power, however revolutionary, had to be paid for. The payment required restoration of the export sector, which required restoration of the sugar economy under a no-nonsense work discipline.

In time this wise if harsh policy yielded to a complicated peasant counterrevolution, which, under the guise of ending dictatorship and tyranny, resulted in the division of the land among war-weary and land-hungry ex-slaves. The ex-slaves then slipped into a subsistence economy, with the tragic outcome so familiar to us and so alluring to white-supremist propagandists.

The experience of the great revolution in St.-Domingue remains arresting, notwithstanding its sad fate. It was the first and only slave revolution in world history. Prior to St.-Domingue all slave revolts, from those of the Roman Empire to the massive risings in Jamaica, Guiana, and elsewhere in the Americas, had been defensive—some might even say socially backward-looking. Those movements of groups of slaves—sometimes, thousands at a time—aspired to withdraw from slave society and reconstruct something approaching a premodern, traditional African way of life. Some of the revolts were successful. Thus, rebel blacks in the interior of Jamaica ("Maroons") forced the British to sign peace treaties guaranteeing their autonomy; thus, rebel blacks in Surinam ("Bush Negroes") secured similar conditions. Thus, smaller groups won autonomy in the Spanish colonies, on the Franco-Spanish border of Santo Domingo and elsewhere. And in Brazil during the seventeenth century, the great colony of runaway slaves called Palmares held out against Dutch and Portuguese troops for most of the century and built a community of about 20,000 people before being overwhelmed by superior force.

In St.-Domingue, however, despite the eventual peasant counterrevolution, the revolt passed into a national revolution aimed not at restoring a lost African world but in building a modern black state. Toussaint's great slogan "free and French" meant that the people of the new state were to have personal freedom under a bourgeois idea of private property within an international community of modern, civilized, interdependent nation-states. Toussaint caught, in those three simple words, the essence of a historical epoch. It had fallen to the people of France to demonstrate that the worldwide cause of popular liberation had crystallized in a single nation, the revolutionary transformation of which provided not so much the model as the inspiration and example to all others.

But Toussaint's vision projected something else as well—something that exposed the world's men of power as paper tigers, that exposed the ultimate hollowness of all grand schemes to unite reactionaries in an invincible phalanx against which oppressed peoples have no chance for victory, that exposed the fundamental stupidity displayed by the best educated classes in their ultimately pathetic attempt to impose their will upon the world. What Toussaint saw was that the world was becoming one, not in the romantic sense so dear to daydreamers who are forever getting themselves beaten in preposterous schemes for some meaningless abstraction of world brotherhood, but in the coldly rational sense that a world economy was emerging, and with it a world political community within which no people could isolate itself.

The apparently unshakable power of the French *colons* of St.-Domingue, like that of their arrogant counterparts in modern Algeria and Vietnam, crumbled under blows delivered by the despised and wretched of the earth. But the critical and most ironical feature of the successful challenge mounted from below was not the impressive power put together by a previously dispirited people, but the superior intelligence and grasp of the course of world events they displayed.

Consider the contrast. The slaveholders believed, contrary to all reason and blatant fact, that they could survive forever in a world in which a liberal opposition was rising to power as a new ruling class on the basis of a theory and practice of bourgeois property demanding free labor as its *sine qua non*. They sought to endure in a world in which the political victory of the middle classes could be slowed and compromised but no longer prevented, in a world in which the liberal ideas of the Enlightment— ideas of individual freedom and dignity steadily being reshaped into a democratic ethos—could no longer be arrested. The slaves who turned revolutionaries in St.-Domingue—or at least their wisest and best, if sometimes illiterate, leaders—knew that the world was being changed utterly and that their hopes depended upon participation as equals in international bourgeois property relations, upon respect for the rights of individuals, and upon a politically viable combination of democratic mass participation and a stern new formulation of political discipline and social order.

After the revolution in St.-Domingue everything changed. The old struggle for power continued, but in decisively new forms. Some of the greatest slave revolts followed—the largest slave revolt in southern history near New Orleans in 1811, the massive rising of thousands in Demerara in 1823, the bloody conjuncture in 1831 of the Nat Turner revolt in Virginia and the historic Christmas rising in Jamaica, the long series of revolts from 1807 to 1835 in Bahia, Brazil, which culminated in a near successful bloodbath, the successful revolutionary general strike in the Danish Virgin Islands in 1848 which provoked a decree of emancipation, the complex movement of blacks into the revolutionary movements of Spanish America and Brazil, and finally in the United States and Brazil the massive participation of blacks, in both violent and nonviolent forms, in broader struggles for emancipation and national reconstruction. These movements had different contents and significance in time and place, and cannot be homogenized to fit some ideological schema. But taken together, they marked a fateful departure from the pattern of slave revolts before the conflagration in St.-Domingue. In one way or another they represented the irrevocable entrance of the slaves and black people generally into world history. No longer did they aspire to tragic and ultimately impossible withdrawals from the one world that the expanding capitalist marketplace was creating. Rather, each movement, with whatever degree of coherence and consciousness, aspired to earn a place for black people in a modern nation-state—one either black and autonomous or sufficiently flexible and tolerant to permit blacks to live on terms of equality with whites. Those struggles have not yet been won even in the United States, but their forward movement, notwithstanding defeats and temporary reverses, has been unmistakable.

With secondary exceptions, these mass movements of slaves and black freedmen supported the forces of liberalism and democracy throughout the Americas. For the moment consider the role these black struggles played in the wider struggle for bourgeois freedom and democracy in the European and Euro-American world. C. L. R. James in his great book *Black Jacobins* delineated this radicalizing effect of the revolution in St.-Domingue on the French Revolution. Gary Nash and Duncan MacLeod only recently have sensitively explored the impact of slavery and racial struggle on the background and course of the revolutionary era in America. Philip Curtin and Mary Reckord have suggested the impact of Jamaican slave revolt on the decisive political reforms in England, much as George Rudé and Eric Hobsbawm have drawn attention to the importance of the agrarian risings at home. John Lynch, in his admirable book on the Spanish American Revolutions, has given the role of the blacks the attention it has long deserved, and a brilliant generation of scholars have been telling the story of the black contribution to emancipation and national reconstruction in Brazil. More literature could be cited, but it ought to be enough to point to the crowning synthesis at the expert hands of David Brion Davis.

The story now unfolding is the story W. E. B. Du Bois long ago predicted would unfold once the historical record could be read without ethnic and elitist blinders. It reveals more than the contribution of black people to their own liberation, which would seem important enough when we recall how few years ago it was being denied and ridiculed. The story also reveals the critical participation of black peoples in the making of the modern world, their extraordinary cultural achievements even as slaves and the place of their struggle for freedom and dignity in the swelling worldwide movement for democracy and social justice. Without the slave revolts and black participation in national liberation and reform movements, reaction would have scored greater triumphs than it did and might have rolled back those forces for change which have shaped the twentieth century. But, clearly, even short of such claims, the worldwide liberal and democratic movements would have had a much harder time and the forces of reaction much better prospects.

I have here argued that the early spread of capitalism called forth a new system of slavery which in time proved economically, politically, and morally incompatible with the consolidation of a capitalist world order and that the slaveholders who arose in the New World increasingly played a role analogous to that of the great lords of Europe in trying to contain the advance of the very capitalist system that had spawned them. I have noted that during the nineteenth century the national bourgeoisies of Europe and the United States, however unevenly, triumphed over these reactionary classes and that, increasingly, the older landed classes passed into the ranks of the bourgeoisie as its extreme right wing. I have also argued that the revolutionary and even reformist movements among the slaves, like the great peasant revolts of Europe and elsewhere, played an indispensable role in launching the worldwide democratic movement that culminated in the rise of socialism.

But, taken together, the two sides of this single process of historical development have added up to a tragedy, not only for ourselves but for those who come after us. The great hope of the bourgeois revolutions of the eighteenth century, most admirably our own, was the reconciliation of individual liberty based on freedom of property with democracy and social justice. Yet, the revolutionary bourgeoisie that brought this magnificent vision into the world could not lay the material foundations for its triumph without washing its hands in the blood of millions and creating a worldwide social and racial chasm. Increasingly, it yielded to the authoritarian and oppressive tendencies of the older classes it had defeated and absorbed. Increasingly, it contributed, with or without deliberate intent, to the divorce of the idea of freedom from the commitment to democracy and social justice.

Simultaneously, those who arose to challenge the bourgeois order from the Left have had to face the realities of their many Haitis. Again, historical analogies should not be pressed too far. But it is hard to resist seeing in Josef Stalin a man who combined Toussaint's vision with Dessalines' single-minded ruthlessness and who successfully demonstrated that cruelty and mass murder can be put to revolutionary as well as conservative uses.

Today the divorce between the ideas of bourgeois freedom and proletarian social justice is nearly complete. Their remarriage in a world of grotesque inequalities, racial hatreds, and fearful new weapons of violence has poor prospects. Yet, the vision of civilization inherent in the original marriage remains America's finest gift to the world. And we Americans may console ourselves that the burden of slavery and racism, and of the subsequent imperialism to which they contributed, has not yet proven insurmountable here at home, has not yet forced us down the road of alternative totalitarianisms. Choices do remain, always provided that we have the wisdom and courage to have done once and for all with the racial oppression and class exploitation that have poisoned our national life and have split us so dangerously from the overwhelming majority of the world's peoples.

Slavery and the American Mind

DAVID BRION DAVIS

The subject "Slavery and the American Mind" requires some preliminary remarks on American ideals and American realities. To the modern ear these words immediately suggest hypocrisy. No one needs to be reminded, for example, that the author of the Declaration of Independence was himself dependent on the labor of some 200 black slaves. Even in 1776 this moral absurdity drew fire from Tory critics and from a few English liberals otherwise sympathetic to the rebels' cause. "If there be an object truly ridiculous in nature," wrote Thomas Day, "it is an American patriot, signing resolutions of independency with the one hand, and with the other brandishing a whip over his affrighted slaves." A few years later Richard Price observed that "it is self-evident [he doubtless used Jefferson's phrase with deliberation] that if there are any men whom they have a right to enslave, there may be others who have had a right to hold them in slavery." In America a few informed blacks and a few white abolitionists drew attention to the discrepancy between ideals and reality. Yet most white Americans either failed to perceive the inconsistency or rationalized it as one of the unavoidable facts of life.

Indeed, one may assume that if the Revolution's leaders had shared the viewpoint of Day and Price, they would not have chosen a wealthy Virginia slaveholder to write the Declaration of Independence, or at least that Jefferson himself would have qualified his appeals to man's inalienable rights. My initial point is

51

simply that the tension between ideals and reality can take a variety of forms. The American mind long handled the problem of slavery by the familiar device of denial. Thus the Constitution transmuted slaves into ghostly "other persons," "such persons," and persons "held to service or labour." It is well known that southern masters frequently referred to slaves as "servants" or as their "people." Henry Hughes, a scholarly young lawyer in Port Gibson, Mississippi, contended that American slavery should really be termed warranteeism, since it protected the servant from violence, hunger, and economic insecurity in exchange for an obligation to work. As E. N. Elliot wrote, "The person of the slave is not property, no matter what the fictions of the law may say. . . . Nor is the labor of the slave solely for the benefit of the master, but for the benefit of all concerned; for himself, to repay the advances made for his support in childhood, for present subsistence, and for guardianship and protection, and to accumulate a fund for sickness, disability, and old age." Warranteeism, it should be stressed, was an ideal. The proslavery writers were notoriously adept at disguising the realities of Negro slavery, but they were generally aware that those realities left much to be desired. Their solution to this problem, reflecting the spirit of much American idealism, was to reform and rename the institution in order to strengthen it. As Eugene D. Genovese and William K. Scarborough have amply demonstrated, the more responsible minds in the South increasingly urged that slavery be ameliorated in accordance with Christian and paternalistic ideals.

One of the cardinal fallacies of intellectual history is to picture ideals as timeless and autonomous forms. All too frequently the historian contents himself with exclamations over the discovery that practice has been inconsistent with professed ideals. Yet all idealism is compromised by tactical expediency, and all opportunism, no matter how ruthless, is compromised and rationalized by ideals. Self-conscious hypocrisy is an ephemeral state of mind. In moments of defiance and rebellion, certain groups may flaunt a moral inconsistency, shouting out, in effect, "So what?" But this stance itself soon becomes transmuted into self-righteous defense or into a more elaborate ideology.

When the historian thinks of ideals and reality as separate and independent spheres of being, he imagines that a conflict between the two must have given rise to guilt. Or to put it another way, he imagines that he would have suffered from guilt if he had been a slaveholder who believed in the rights of man. But many historians, like most novelists, tend to exaggerate the guilt that various villains are supposed to feel. Guilt is after all a most reassuring and conservative concept, expressing at once an inner conviction of wrongdoing and an external conviction, by judicial process, of objective crime. The correspondence between conscience and social norms is obviously the basis for moral order. One should recall, however, that while Mark Twain's Huck Finn was only half-civilized, his conscience echoed the norms of the antebellum South; he therefore felt genuine guilt over extending the slightest aid and encouragement to a fugitive slave. As Twain acutely saw, especially in the pessimism of his later years, conscience and social norms can be powerful engines of self-deception. For the historian the key questions should not involve contradictions between ideals and reality, but rather should deal with the social uses of moral compromise. What is truly terrifying is not inconsistency and hypocrisy but social self-deception. And if history is to be one of the arts by which we gain a truer knowledge of ourselves, we need unusual honesty whenever we examine the relationship between ideals and certain lethal patterns of behavior that have developed through acts of unconscious and self-deceiving compromise.

Perhaps I should clarify what I mean by the relationship between ideals and lethal social systems. Some years ago I wrote a chapter on what seemed a momentous historical paradox—that, given the lack of an alternative labor supply, it is difficult to see how European nations could have settled the New World and exploited its resources without the aid of African slaves. From the time of the first discoveries and settlements, slavery was an intrinsic part of the American experience. Yet the settlement of the New World inspired utopian dreams of boundless opportunity, of human perfectibility, and of historical progress. For many Europeans, America became a symbol of uncorrupted nature, a terrestrial paradise that promised fulfillment of man's highest aspirations. Insofar as the New World impinged on the thought of the Renaissance and Enlightenment, it encouraged a moral vision totally antithetical to chattel slavery. But this moral vision drew nourishment from the tangible success of America and thus from the continuing extension of chattel slavery.

If I were to rewrite the chapter today, I should try to highlight a number of ignored or slighted points. First, for well over a century prior to the discovery of America, the extension of slavery and the slave trade had been integral parts of European commercial expansion in the Mediterranean and eastern Atlantic, and had thus been associated with the most progressive, enlightened, and cosmopolitan societies. Among the many institutions that Christians and Jews borrowed and adapted from Islamic societies was Negro slavery, which began to take root in Sicily, the Iberian peninsula, and the Atlantic sugar islands before Columbus discovered America. In other words, Europe's initial exploitation of African labor was a product of the same forces that led to widening economic opportunity, to the production of sugar and other luxuries for international markets, and to the moral and cultural aspirations of an urban, bourgeois culture. In this connection one should note the pioneering role of Italian merchants in developing sugar plantations in Madeira, the regular shipment of slave-grown Madeiran sugar to England, and the role of Dutch and Flemish capitalists in promoting sugar plantations in the Atlantic islands and then in Brazil.

A second point is that the economic development of the New World depended on the dispossession of its native inhabitants and on the introduction of a disciplined labor force of African origin. On this question perceptions have long been dulled by the coercions of topical compartments. Specialists in Afro-American history seldom mention Indians; the now fashionable interest in Indians points to an autonomous field of study and sometimes even to a competitive replacement for the depleting interest in Negro slavery. There are no comparative studies of the repeated European attempts to enslave Indians, or of the relation between the treatment of Indians and the massive importation of black slaves. We have only begun to appreciate the extent to which the history of New World slavery may have turned on the disease environment of the West African coast (which long prevented European settlement), on the relative healthfulness of the New World for both Europeans and Africans, and on the extraordinary vulnerability of Indians to Old World diseases which rapidly annihilated vast populations from the West Indies to the interior of the two continents. Although the standard texts make reference to Bartolomé de Las Casas's proposal to the Spanish crown, in about 1518, urging that Negro slaves be substituted for the Arawak laborers who were dying at an alarming rate in the mines of Hispaniola, there has been little recognition that the extension of sugar and slaves was everywhere preceded by the extermination, subjugation, or removal of aborigines. This sequence of events was as important in Brazil as in the Caribbean. In the few regions where the Arawak mounted effective resistance, such as Dominica, St. Vincent, and the Guyanese coast, the plantation system was long in taking root.

Despite the extensive and valuable work that has been done on racial attitudes, literary primitivism, and kindred subjects, much is yet to be learned about the intertwined fate of Indians and Negro slaves. Literary histories discuss the links between Daniel Defoe's image of savagery and his new ideal of the self-sufficient man, but often fail to note that Robinson Crusoe had been a successful

Brazilian planter who, at the time of his shipwreck, was bound for West Africa in search of slaves. A number of students of literary primitivism have commented on the remarkable interchangeability of noble red Apollos and sable African princes. But no one, so far as I know, has asked whether the generally more favorable European image of the Amerind was influenced by the fact that Amerinds, reeling from a tidal wave of epidemics, appeared quite literally to be a perishing race. This image may have contributed to the continuing efforts of the Spanish and Portuguese governments to protect Indians from being enslaved. These efforts were only partially successful, but they stand in marked contrast to the virtually unquestioned official policy of promoting the spread of Negro slavery.

The comparative studies of slavery in British and Latin America have said surprisingly little about Indians, although the differences in Amerind cultures and population densities must have constituted an important variable. In Latin America, millions of Indians perished from disease, forced labor, and sheer slaughter. But no one could have conceived of physically removing the Indians from an area equivalent in size to the entire United States from the Atlantic to the Mississippi River. By the end of the War of 1812, however, only an estimated 125,000 Indians inhabited that immense region of North America. It is too often forgotten that the creation of the Cotton Kingdom depended on Andrew Jackson's decisive defeat of the Creeks, on the removal of the last lingering danger of an alliance between Indians and a European ally, and on the final eviction of the five civilized tribes from some of the richest lands of the South. The government's success in dispossessing the southern tribes led directly to the frenzied land speculation in Alabama and Mississippi and to the great cotton boom of the late 1820s and early 1830s. Although there is still much debate over the effect of this boom on national economic growth, it clearly attracted foreign investment capital and produced the raw material that supplied the leading industry of the Northeast, that paid as an export for the major share of imports, and that supported the structure of national credit.

Even in 1770 the Abbé Raynal contemplated the butchery and enslavement resulting from the discovery of America and questioned whether the human costs justified the new promise to mankind. To the familiar excuse that the lands of the New World could not be cultivated without slaves, he replied: "Well, then, let them lie fallow, if it means that to make these lands productive, man must be reduced to brutishness, whether he be the man who buys, or he who sells, or he who is sold." But one cannot take seriously such rhetorical flourishes of despair, either from the *philsosphes* or from their more pragmatic North American successors. For the liberal mind there were no social or moral problems that could not be solved by progress and material growth. Who could doubt that in the long run the Indians' best interest would be served by discouraging a primitive and inefficient use of land which the Creator had obviously intended for cultivation and for the support of a large and prosperous population? Who could doubt that the descendants of African savages would ultimately benefit from the fruits of their own productivity, coupled with the blessings of Christian civilization?

This commitment to material progress brings me to a further point. In the United States, both the removal of Indians and the extension of Negro slavery helped to prepare the way for the triumph of a market-oriented society. Modern economists tend to describe the emergence of a market economy as an unmixed blessing and as the prerequisite for all social progress. Although the texts say little about Indians, one discovers the following passage in a recent collaborative history by distinguished cliometricians, "[A] certain competent greediness for material objects is needed if economies are to 'go.' The American Indian consumed less than $10 per person in trade goods as late as the 1830s. He showed little willingness to shift to the new American mode of existence—a shift so necessary if more and ever more goods were to be acquired." The Indian, we are half-humorously reassured, was far from being an ascetic noble savage; he "valued the products of the distillery and the armory no less than his successors." Unfortunately for him, however, he lacked the essential qualifications for American civilization. The Indian "showed little interest in material accumulation, and hence failed to use his energies in ways that induced output increases, that created measured economic growth." *

It is enlightening to contrast this judgment with the attempt by Professors Robert Fogel and Stanley Engerman to prove that black slaves were efficient workers who internalized the Protestant work ethic. If the Indian was a lost cause from the very beginning, the black slave in Fogel and Engerman's view at least increased output, contributed to measured economic growth, and acquired the competent greediness for material objects that equipped him for a responsible role in a market society. Unlike the Indian, the Negro became a cooperative and productive partner in progress. The economic system—as distinct from the anomaly of slavery—is thus vindicated from the charge of intrinsic injustice.

Yet the moral contradiction, I submit, not only remains but appears more disturbing the more it is honestly scrutinized. From the late Middle Ages, Europeans increasingly associated man's progress toward liberty with the expansion of commerce and the hegemony of market relationships. Just prior to the discovery of America, slaves were being sought less as symbols of luxury and prestige, as in most of the Islamic world, and more as the producers of commodities like sugar that were highly valued by the European bourgeoisie. It was this labor intensive system that provided the key to developing the resources of the New World, once the inefficient Indian economies had been displaced. And while the concentration on subtropical staples helped to extend market relationships—the specialization in the West Indies, for

* Stanley Lebergott, "The American Labor Force," in *America's Economic Growth: An Economists' History of the United States*, eds. Lance E. Davis, et al. (New York, 1972), 184–85.

example, allowed the northern colonies to specialize in exporting provisions, horses, lumber, and other commodities—the most concentrated and organized sectors of labor remained insulated from market forces except when the owners or prospective owners of labor responded to such forces. The removal of North American Indians and the extension of slavery into the Old Southwest became the foundation for spectacular economic growth that seemed to benefit everyone (everyone, that is, who was both free and willing to shift to what economists term "the new American mode of existence"). But this was a freedom purchased by some at the cost of others, and in this case the some were white and the others were not.

Thus far I have purposefully refrained from mentioning race, although I quickly acknowledge that in the American mind race has always been the central reality of slavery. Indeed, Americans have assumed that the relationship is obvious and self-evident, a confident assurance that should always arouse suspicion. The conventional questions rest on the assumption that white Americans restricted slavery to Negroes, and go on from there to consider the origins and consequences of racial prejudice. But during much of the colonial period, North American laws gave sanction to Indian slavery although the laws protected the liberty of Indian allies and other friendly tribes. By the early nineteenth century virtually all persons held as slaves were arbitrarily defined as Negroes, regardless of the fact that large numbers of these slaves had Indian and European ancestry. Race, with respect to Negro slavery, was clearly a label imposed by white society. As John Blassingame has pointed out, American slaves developed their own color distinctions which often expressed disgust or shame over white ancestry. But these attitudes would surely have been different, though not necessarily less hostile, if all mulattoes had been freed and accorded a distinct and semiprivileged status. Both the concept and definition of Negro were the products of history and culture.

Winthrop Jordan has richly documented the history of racial

fears and stereotypes that preceded the institutionalization of Negro slavery in British America—prejudices that drew continuing nourishment from circumstances independent of slavery. More recently, Bernard Lewis has uncovered similar racial stereotypes in Islamic literature of the Middle Ages. And Carl Degler has contrasted the rigid North American dichotomy between black and white with the Latin American range of color distinctions, suggesting that in Brazil a "mulatto escape hatch" kept racial relations from polarizing as in the United States. One can accept the importance of culture in shaping racial perceptions and still propose the novel possibility that racial attitudes had more underlying significance in Latin America than in the United States. Professor Degler's own evidence shows that white Brazilians—and the point can be extended to Spanish Americans—were far more sensitive than British Americans to the physical appearance of people of mixed ancestry. The Latin Americans officially recognized differing mixtures of red, black, and white. The elaborate taxonomy of physical types, linked with differences in status, treatment, and opportunity, suggests the dominance of racial consciousness. The familiar observation that North Americans defined anyone with visible African ancestry as a Negro has been taken as proof of an even more blatant racial consciousness. That it expressed a blatant form of racism, as that term is now understood, no one can deny. What has too often been overlooked, however, is that the institution of slavery took precedence over racial loyalty. By classifying as black a slave who was seven-eighths white, North Americans ensured the security of private property at the expense of racial sensitivity.

My argument presupposes that private property was a more central value in North America than in Latin America, and that North Americans had more fully internalized a commitment to material accumulation, output increases, and measured economic growth. But what, one may ask, of the North Americans' notorious obsession with theories of racial inferiority? Clearly this is a question of infinite complexity, as the studies of Professors Jordan, Degler, Frederickson, and others have amply demonstrated. Here I can do no more than call attention to an often neglected consequence or theories of biological inferiority.

By emphasizing the supposed taint of African blood, carrying with it the supposedly savage and undisciplined instincts of prehistoric man, North Americans could affirm a belief in the incapacity of all slaves, regardless of outward appearance, to respond to the incentives of a market society. The ideology of race could thus justify the anomaly of slavery in a capitalistic setting, diverting attention from the actual dependence of the free market on coerced labor. What I have termed a lethal system could be disguised in two ways. First, racial theory defined persons of African ancestry as essentially living fossils, as the representatives of a stage of evolution in which forced labor was the only means of production and social discipline. In this view the introduction of Africans had also introduced a different historical mode of being which had to coexist with progressive capitalism. This thought helps illuminate the desire to deport free blacks and to manumit and colonize slaves, if slavery could be shown to have outlived its economic usefulness. Like the parallel removal of Eastern Indians, the proposed expulsion of blacks had a temporal as well as spatial dimension. Neither group, according to racist doctrine, was capable of adjusting to a modern age in which universal freedom required the rational choices of a market-oriented personality. The second deception was that the obsession with race cloaked the continuing dependence of the economy on slave labor. In confronting the contradictions between ideals and reality, it was easier for the American mind to dwell on the Negro's alleged incapacity for freedom than to acknowledge the national interests served by his bondage.

This interpretation, which by no means excludes a host of other variables, receives indirect support from the curious nature of American debates over emancipation. The abolitionists' debates focused on the abstract legality and morality of slavery, on the undeniable barbarities of the system, and on the capabilities of the Negro people. It is true that the legislatures of the northern states, when drafting laws for gradual emancipation, showed an acute concern for property rights, for labor discipline, and for apportioning the costs of emancipation. Professors Fogel and Engerman have shown in a recent essay that these lawmakers skillfully contrived to eliminate or minimize the capital losses of slaveholders and to make northern slaves pay the major cost of their own emancipation. This discovery highlights the strange air of unreality that characterized the later national controversies over slavery in the South. Let me emphasize that I am not simply repeating the old charge that abolitionists were obsessed with guilt and abstract justice. As radical reformers it was their business to shatter complacency and expose self-serving and self-deceiving compromise. They understood that whatever moral power they exerted could only be dissipated by disputes over the most practicable means of emancipation. What is striking is that the abolitionists' ideals were countered by a definition of reality that virtually excluded questions of cost, productivity, resources, and national interest. The hard facts of life which supposedly precluded or required the indefinite postponement of emancipation were the alleged facts of race—the Negro's incapacity to behave as a responsible economic man, and the threat that racial intermixture, unless the offspring were quietly plowed back into the slave population, would spread the contamination of brutish, impulse-ridden, and premodern behavior.

Unfortunately, the abolitionists had no means of escaping the snares of this ideology even if they had perceived them. It would have been self-defeating to point out that the insuperable and unacknowledged obstacles to emancipation lay at the heart of American society—in the reliance of the national economy on slave labor, in the steadily rising value of slave property, and in the weakness of any countervailing force, supported as in Britain by an alliance of aristocratic traditions and new economic interests independent of political ties with a planter class. Moreover, from the time of the Revolution, American abolitionists had actually reinforced the primacy of race since they had continuously faced the need of proving that blacks were not inherently inferior to whites. The circumstances of debate had forced them to stoop to the level of apologizing for the supposed shortcomings of African civilization and of parading specimens of individual black achievement. No matter how gifted, these embarrassed black poets and scholars were always highly vulnerable, particularly since their defenders took on something of the role of P. T. Barnums displaying curiosities—that is, blacks who could think and speak like whites.

This impresario role was something more than a response to racial prejudice. Abolitionism, in England as well as in America, became one of the prongs of a vast missionary crusade intended to universalize the virtues of self-improvement, sobriety, conscientious work, and fiscal responsibility, thereby bringing all humanity under the literal government of a Protestant God. In both countries abolitionist leaders tended to be seasoned veterans of organizations for various kinds of moral improvement—societies for spreading Christian tracts, for educating the poor, for promoting savings banks and the observance of the Christian sabbath, for suppressing vice, intemperance, lotteries, and vulgar amusements. Abolitionists could strive to redeem all men from the physical dominion of other men precisely because they believed in the ideal of moral responsibility. They were confident that every individual, when freed from physical constraints, had the ability to behave as a responsible moral agent, choosing virtue much as Adam Smith's ideal economic man would choose efficiency and productivity in response to the incentives and punishments of the free market.

In answer to the racism that excluded nonwhites from the

benefits of the free market, the abolitionists opposed an evangelical faith in immediate conversion. The great message of evangelical Protestantism had collapsed all historical stages into an urgent and limitless NOW; the inhabitants of Burma, China, and the Mississippi valley were all ripe for salvation. It was not by accident that so many future abolitionists spoke out against Indian removal or that their anger over Georgia's incarceration of missionaries preceded the heated conflict over deluging the South with abolitionist mail. But this desire to redeem the American system by reducing its exploitive and discriminatory costs depended on the hope of rehabilitating its victims. New Englanders rejoiced over the news of the Cherokees' schoolhouses, Bibles, and printing press; and they later expressed happy astonishment over Frederick Douglass' native eloquence. The difficulty was that most white Americans did not want civilized Indians and eloquent ex-slaves; they wanted the Indians' land and the Negroes' labor.

The militant abolitionism of the 1830s embodied an unseen contradiction that was related both to the uncertain realities of American society and to the illusion that the same principles and determination that had triumphed in Great Britain would have similar consequences in the radically different social structure of Jacksonian America. On one level, the abolitionists realistically saw that the nation had reached a dead end on the question of slavery. Instead of gradually withering away, as earlier optimists had hoped, the evil had grown and had won increasing acquiescence from the nation's political leaders and most powerful institutions. Therefore, the abolitionists took on the unpopular role of radical agitators standing outside the popular refuges of delusion, hypocrisy, and rationalization. Led by William Lloyd Garrison, they took up the free blacks' grievances against the American Colonization Society and against the discriminatory laws and customs of the northern states, which reinforced slavery by denying free blacks the chance to prove their capability for freedom. But having virtually declared war against the values, institutions, and power structure of Jacksonian America, the abolitionists continued to think of their societies as simple extensions of the so-called Benevolent Empire—that galaxy of nondenominational organizations modeled chiefly on British precedents. They assumed that they could quickly win support from churches and ministers and that they could persuade the pious, influential, and respectable community leaders that racial prejudice was as harmful as intemperance. After mobilizing righteous opinion in the North, they could then shame the South into repentance.

The history of antislavery illustrates the truth that what may appear as benign change in one social setting becomes revolutionary in another. Ironically, Americans had failed to appreciate the explosiveness of their own republican ideology when exported to aristocratic and tradition-oriented societies. In 1832 and 1833, American reformers failed to appreciate that the British emancipation movement could never have won the support of the established order and of middleclass public opinion in Britain if it had endangered any vital national interest. Or to phrase it more acurately, American abolitionists could not perceive that in the United States slavery was a vital national interest and that they were directly challenging the network of compromises and self-deceptions by which the nation had disguised an unpleasant reality. They could not think of themselves as revolutionaries; by historical definition, in America as well as Britain, the evangelical conscience was supposed to be an antidote to revolution. These abolitionists did not think of themselves as provokers of violence and disunion. They insisted, rather, that it was slavery that had brought increasing violence and that a national commitment to emancipation would ensure harmony and national union.

These expectations help to explain the pained outrage, the shrill rhetoric, and the self-righteous courage that led American abolitionists beyond the last boundaries of permissible dissent. To their dismay, they discovered that disinterested benevolence aroused only hatred and violence, that the courage to speak the truth provoked attempts at intimidation and suppression. The leadership of such wealthy philanthropists as Arthur and Lewis Tappan did not lend respectability to the cause, as in Britain; it rather led to mobs that gutted Lewis Tappan's New York City house and to promised rewards in the South for $50,000 in return for Arthur Tappan's body. In striking back at the abolitionists, the northern colonizationists fully exploited their most dangerous weapon—their enemies, they made clear, were "amalgamationists" who would not stop short of encouraging black men to woo the daughters of white America. It was this bugaboo that brought the northern crowds into the streets.

The abolitionists failed in their determination to make American ideals transform American reality. Yet by stubbornly defending and reinvigorating ideals, they elicited a response that exposed some of the uglier truths of American existence. In this sense they shattered what today has come to be called a consensus, the conviction, which even Garrison originally shared, that the nation was basically sound and that reformers could count on the public's good will, patriotism, and Christian conscience. The resulting disillusion contributed to the Garrisonians' radical repudiation of all institutional limits imposed by the threat of force. In the eyes of the New England radicals, Negro slavery and racial oppression were merely extreme manifestations of an evil embodied in the patriarchal family, in the criminal law, and in the police power of the state. This ideology of nonresistance moved far beyond the doctrines of the Benevolent Empire and of British abolitionism; indeed, the Garrisonians exerted considerable influence on the history of British dissent, particularly in the provinces. It is a mistake to judge the Garrisonians by the ordinary pragmatic criteria of American reform. For their significance lies in discovering a moral vantage point which at least partly transcended their society and which forced that society to define its boundaries of tolerance and of freedom of speech.

Yet ultimately abolitionism gravitated toward the normal

American channels of pragmatic adjustment. The movement fragmented as a result of the diverse and confused responses to the violent anger of the 1830s. But the resulting division into various political and antipolitical factions amounted to a diversification of product that eased the assimilation of antislavery ideas into northern society. Since there was no common party line, northerners were free to choose the brand of abolitionism that suited them best. In this respect Garrison's disavowal of politics served the important function of legitimizing antislavery politics, since one could vote for a Liberty party or Liberty League candidate without risk of being tainted by Garrisonian radicalism.

It is not surprising that this dilution of purpose worked against the interests of northern free blacks. Black conventions had led the way in denouncing the colonization society. Black abolitionists had given Garrison's *Liberator* its major support and had worked closely with antislavery societies in New England and New York. During the 1840s, fugitive slaves began the indispensable task of translating the abolitionists' abstract images into concrete human experience. The lectures and printed narratives of Frederick Douglass, William Wells Brown, Ellen Craft, Henry Bibb, and a host of others did much to undermine northern beliefs that slaves were kindly treated and contented with their lot. Yet when Douglass and Garrison traveled together on lecture tours, it was Douglass who experienced constant insult, humiliation, and harrassment. Black vigilance committees could help a small number of fugitives find their way to Canada and relative security, but, except in Massachusetts, black abolitionists had little leverage for loosening the rock-like edifice of discriminatory law. Indeed, white abolitionists kept pressuring blacks to keep a low profile, to act the part assigned them by white directors (who presumably knew the tastes of an all-white audience), and to do nothing that might spoil the show.

If abolitionism gradually became more acceptable in the North, it was for a price that confirmed the white abolitionists' fears of racism as well as the resulting powerlessness of their black allies. Many blacks increasingly resented the attention given to women's rights, nonresistance, and communitarian experiments, and the almost conspiratorial caution that immobilized the question of racial equality in the North. They also resented the patronizing attitudes of white abolitionists who might defend abstract equality while treating blacks as inferiors who had to be led. Black abolitionists generally looked to voting, a right few blacks possessed, as the most promising route to power. For the most part, therefore, they supported the Liberty party in 1840 and 1844 and the Free-Soil party in 1848. The drift of antislavery politics, however, was toward the lowest common denominator, or away from black civil rights in the north and emancipation in the southern states. Although the Free-Soil convention welcomed black delegates, the platform, unlike that of the Liberty party, ignored the question of legal discrimination. It is not surprising that by 1854 a few black leaders were talking of a separate black nation, or that blacks who had proudly defended their American heritage and right to American citizenship were beginning to reconsider the question of voluntary colonization.

I have tried to approach the question of slavery and the American mind by examining the relationship between ideals and certain lethal patterns of behavior that developed through acts of unconscious and self-deceiving compromise. Unfortunately, the way Americans resolved the problem of slavery adds force to the argument that social self-deceptions have generally been overcome only by further self-deceptions. No one could have convinced the northern people that the institution of slavery had been an inseparable part of Western Europe's commercial and imperial expansion, that it had played an even more central role in the economic development of the United States, and that doctrines of racial inferiority had served to disguise the exploitation of blacks by whites as well as the contribution of blacks to America's economic viability. Yet by the 1850s many northerners were prepared to believe that the institution of slavery had created a southern oligarchy, the Slave Power, that threatened to seize permanent control of the American government. The North's romantic ideals—embodied in the aspirations of the Benevolent Empire, of the religious revivalists, and of the evangelical reformers—could be focused in a great crusade to keep the western territories free, to confine and seal in the Slave Power, and thus open the way for a supposed expansion of righteous liberty and opportunity that would transcend all worldly limits. This was the kind of vision that could appeal at least to a significant number of northerners who were prepared to resist the Slave Power without believing either that slaveholding was sinful or that free blacks had a right to legal equality.

Without the abolitionists, slavery would never have emerged as a moral problem. But the abolitionists finally won a hearing by dramatizing a supposedly irreconcilable conflict between the interests and cultures of North and South—not by generating a will in the North to cross the ideological borders that blocked the way to the emancipation of the slaves and to social justice.

The Southern Slave Economy

STANLEY L. ENGERMAN[1]

The economics of slavery and the nature of the slave economy have long been discussed and debated. They were subjects of concern even in Greek and Roman times, and the evaluation of the slave economy has long continued to be a topic of interest to historians and economists. To judge from recent discussions, this subject is still capable of generating argument, and in many ways the recent arguments are still about the questions raised in the earlier debates. However, before turning to these debates, let me present some background on the southern economy of a rather noncontroversial nature.

I

The southern economy had, almost from its beginning, combined slave and free labor in an agriculturally based economy. For the most part the free labor population exceeded the slave population, but because of differences in the measured labor force participation rates (mainly due to the exclusion of free women and children from the conventionally defined labor force), the slave agricultural labor force generally exceeded that of whites. And, of course, it is this slave sector which has been the dominant concern, both to contemporaries and to subsequent scholars. Slave labor was concentrated on larger units than the traditional white family farm and was involved in the production of a different set of crops. Not that slave labor did not produce the grains and livestock of the family

71

farms. Rather, slave labor was more frequently used to produce export crops which were grown on only a limited basis on free farms. This export crop varied over time and area. In the eighteenth century, slave labor was used in the production of tobacco in the Upper South, with rice the dominant crop in the coastal areas of South Carolina and Georgia. The start of the nineteenth century saw the major crop shift to short staple cotton, a crop which was capable of being grown throughout the South and which thus permitted a wider geographic spread of slavery than did the earlier crops.

In the period for which such estimates are possible, 1840 to 1860, exports of the staple commodities, mainly cotton, accounted for between 20 and 30 percent of total southern output.[2] This undoubtedly represented some increase over the course of the nineteenth century. Cotton was the major export crop from the South, accounting for about one-quarter of southern agricultural output in 1850. Specialization in other staples persisted. Tobacco, produced in the Upper South, accounted for about 3 percent of southern agricultural output in 1850. Rice, produced in the coastal areas of South Carolina and Georgia, amounted to less than 1 percent, and sugar, produced mainly in Louisiana, accounted for about 5 percent of that year's southern agricultural yield.[3] There was, of course, some use of slave labor in mixed farming, in industry, and in domestic service in various parts of the South. Slave labor, on staple-producing units, was also utilized to produce foodstuffs, to provide capital formation via land-clearing, and to perform various skilled, artisan-type functions. While the average size of slave units increased over time, this was mainly due to geographic shifts rather than to increase in size in given areas.[4] And the size of units throughout the South tended to be considerably smaller than those in the slaveholding areas of the Caribbean, particularly those which specialized in sugar.

Over one-fourth of southern families in 1860 owned slaves, a slight decline over the nineteenth century, although the plantation sector (defining it as over 10 slaves) was restricted to about 7.4 percent of all southern families. Yet these units accounted for about three-quarters of all slaves. (For the more traditional cutoff of 20 slaves, the numbers are about 3 percent of white families and over one-half of the slaves.)[5] Thus, while the larger than family farm units forming the slave economy did not include all slaves, it did contain a substantial majority of them.

The slave population of the South was both rapidly growing and geographically mobile. As noted frequently, it was the one New World slave population which was able to reproduce itself by natural means. A small fraction of total slave imports into North America resulted in a much larger share of New World black population in subsequent years. Philip Curtin estimates that mainland North America received less than 5 percent of all New World slave imports. By 1825, the United States contained over one-third of the New World black population.[6] The principal factor in this increase was the very high rate of U.S. slave fertility, a rate as high as that of the white population of the South. These birth rates were greatly in excess not only of those of other New World slaves, but of all European nations, as well as those of the northern United States. Moreover these high rates of population growth began quite early in settlement and were affected only slightly, if at all, by the cessation of imports due to the Revolution and the final closing of the slave trade in 1808.

Geographic movement westward was a characteristic of the post-Revolutionary era, particularly in the boom years of the 1830s and 1850s. This movement represented primarily an expansion in production of the major staple, cotton, not a shift to any of the other major export crops. To facilitate this expansion, an extensive transport network was developed, the South being among the nation's leaders in the introduction of canals and railways. The South was also able to use several major rivers for transporting goods, inward and outward. The extent of industrial development, however, was relatively small. Some pockets did develop, particularly in Virginia with the use of slave labor in iron and in tobacco, but these paled in comparison with the extensive agricultural sector. As recent work indicates, however, the rates of return to industrial firms using slave labor were quite high in the antebellum period.[7] As a trading area the South used its income from commodity exports to purchase imports, probably foodstuffs from the Midwest in the earlier nineteenth century and then, later, manufactured goods from the East.[8] This pattern, of course, established the South as a crucial link in the national economy during this period and as a major source of foreign exchange, contributing to the American growth process.

There were variations in southern (as in northern) economic performance, with some reversal due to the impact of the Revolutionary War and to the subsequent change in trade patterns. Later there were marked cycles, peaking in the 1830s and late 1850s. The price of slaves reflected cyclical movements, rising to great heights in these periods of boom activity and dropping sharply in the ensuing troughs, though there was generally a rising trend in slave prices in the nineteenth century after the recovery from the post-Revolutionary setback. This increase in price occurred despite the great increase in the supply of slaves in the southern economy; and the ability to move slaves interregionally, by sale or by relocation, meant that similar price patterns were to be found in all areas of the South.

Much more can (and has been) said about the southern economy, both as description and evaluation. Over forty years after its publication, there still is no better single source than Lewis Gray's *History of Agriculture in the Southern United States To 1860* for an examination of the development and evolution of the South's agricultural sector. My reason for such a brief sketch here is that this ample body of material exists, and I wish only to highlight several points as background to the study of the economics of southern slavery.

II

The fact that the economic argument figures so centrally in debates on slavery has, no doubt, presented problems for subsequent writers, creating difficulties in the evaluation of claims
and in the selection of relevant data and evidence. Much of this
earlier discussion, particularly among those attacking the slave
system, was aimed at influencing not only third parties but, more
importantly, the holders of slaves. Therefore, one argument involved reduced stress upon issues concerning the morality of the
system, with emphasis given to the presumed economic unprofitability and inefficiency of slavery. If this seemed unlikely
based on the obvious wealth of slaveholders, it remained possible
to argue that the system of slavery led to an economy and society
which was poorer and worse off for all than would have been a
non-slave society. (Reading these debates makes one wonder why
the notion of counterfactual arguments could raise a stir centuries
later.) In responding to these attacks on the peculiar institution, it
was somewhat inappropriate to argue that the system was being
maintained because it was to the economic interests of the owners.
This would be considered an insufficient and unjustifiable defense,
too coarse and lacking in necessary moral grandeur, at least relative to the defenses of a "higher way of life" and the "need for
control and care of a backward people unfortunately introduced in
previous generations." Of course, some did point to the economic
benefits of slavery, benefits which permitted concentration on
certain crops which might not otherwise have been grown in the
same quantity. But these benefits, it would be argued, went to the
consumers of slave-grown products. This was held to be a rather
crass form of special pleading, even if true. More generally, it
seemed to be held that elimination of slavery would not only be
costless to the nation (including the planters), but would even
yield positive economic benefits.

Moreover, the form that the attack on the slave economy took often led subsequent writers to intertwine two related, but quite different, questions. One relates to the long-term impact of the slave economy, involving projections of its future performance. The other matter, presumably more important to those historians interested in the explanation of social and political events, relates to the patterns perceived by the free (and slave) population of the time. Clearly there is an interaction between the two issues, but a concentration on the first of these, the long-term projections, can be misleading if intended as a description of actual events. Thus, it is often argued that the economic development of the antebellum South was based on a unique configuration of fortuitous economic events, and that the "true" effect of the slave economy was "temporarily" deferred by these. Perhaps this is accurate; indeed under certain conditions it is obviously true. However, to use a frequent comparison, a similar set of fortuitous elements seems to have occurred for various oil producers today. Transient, perhaps, and not itself a basis for long-term development, yet if one tries to understand the timing and nature of events today, to look at the long-run projection and not the short-term condition would be highly misleading. Thus, even if the slavery in the South couldn't survive 1890, or 1920, and was economically backward in some sense, that by itself does not necessarily have implications for what southerners thought in the antebellum years.

On this somewhat methodological ground it might be useful to briefly discuss the nature and varieties of evidence which have been used to study these economic issues. Thus, even if we accept the arguments of some contemporary observers as reflecting reality as they saw it, it is not always easy to evaluate what it means for those questions of interest to historians. In many cases we can find reason enough to explain away what other people (particularly businessmen) say. How many bosses are satisfied with their labor force, and who didn't worry about future production and marketing conditions? And since in any period there are some gainers and some losers, how can we weigh the different sources? Complaints of losers seem more widespread than the self-congratulations of winners, particularly since one of the characteristics of winners is the striving for further improvement. A history of northern agriculture written from Vermont, New Hampshire, or even upstate New York sources in 1860 would look quite different than one written from Midwestern sources. All would be accurate in describing their own area, but we have little difficulty in evaluating the meaning and implication of each when we try to draw an overall picture of northern agriculture. One suspects that similar points might have some bearing upon our evaluation of southern agriculture as well.

Given these brief, skeptical remarks on certain sources, let me turn to a source which economists tend to rely upon but which others often regard more skeptically. This is the information conveyed by studying the movements of prices. Prices are not generally imposed from on high upon an economy, but rather reflect the outcome of decisions made (rightly or wrongly) by a large number of people. These decisions reflect, and prices register, the opinions and impressions of individuals just as much as words do. People will pay higher prices for assets if they expect more earnings in the future, and, of course, these forecasts reflect not just purely economic events, but political, military, and other expected actions as well. Some economists might go so far as to argue that the information conveyed in prices is a more accurate and better presentation of what opinions people have had. After all, purchasing an asset in the market represents a gamble which involves the risk of losing something which most people value rather highly—wealth—while "talk is cheap," and often entered into for the explicit purpose of trying to influence other people. Without going to this extreme, it is useful to remember that price movements convey important information as to what people expect, and are betting on. It would be as unsatisfactory to point to written records or oral polemics as a reason to justify dismissal of the information conveyed by prices as it would be to use the price data to argue that the written and oral statements should be completely ignored. Rather, this difference in evidence points to the need to reconcile a situation in which people are saying one thing and betting on another, a dilemma, such as exists in the interpretation of the late 1850s, reflecting the fact that individuals were apparently generating conflicting impressions and evidence as to their attitudes.

III

There are several ways in which the long historiography of the economics of slavery can be broken down, both as to questions asked and method of analysis. In the past I have presented several such divisions, but I shall return to the one which was used by Ulrich Phillips, and also frequently by the contemporaries in this debate. One set of questions concerns what might be termed private effects, the returns to the slaveowning planter within the system. These involve a study of individual decision-making within an ongoing system, and, given the attempt to convince individual owners of the error of their ways, figured extensively in the contemporary debates. The second type deals with social effects, the evaluation of the overall southern economic performance compared with either some actual economy of the time or else with some hypothetical alternative presumably possible if some other form of labor system was used. Such an evaluation seeks to determine whether the observed southern economic system was "best" from the point of view of long-term income growth and of income distribution among the relevant population. It is really much broader than this, however, since it often entails an analysis of an entire social system, asking what would have been the developments—social, psychological, and political, as well as economic—in the region in the absence of this peculiar form of labor ownership.

One question asked about private effects is that of profitability.

Was the purchase of slaves an investment which yielded, to a planter who purchased (or did not sell) a slave at the market prices of the time, a return equal to the return possible from some alternative use of these funds? More broadly, did it pay to buy slaves from the African trade when that option was open, and after that ended, did it pay to raise newborn slaves until used in production or sold?

A related question is that of the viability of the slave economy as an economic institution. Would the system have become unprofitable and, by further assumption, ended on economic grounds at some time? Here we may note the curious paradox that those historians who seem to be the most extreme economic determinists are not those who are economists or Marxists (occasionally overlapping groups), but rather those such as Craven and Randall who argued that a direct link could be traced from slave prices to profits to the survival of the institution. This is a position which need not be accepted, not only in general, but, more particularly, within the range of prices and profits observed in the immediate pre-Civil War period. The viability question does remain rather difficult for economic historians, since the economic logic clearly indicates the theoretical conditions necessary for slavery to be a losing proposition to owners, conditions which have the curious implication that free labor would be acceptable only when all labor returns were at a subsistence level. These conditions are rather obvious—too much labor relative to land (with no offset in technology or any shift to manufacturing, although such a shift was anticipated by DeBow, among others[9]) or else a fall in product demand (with limited adjustments in producing other goods)— and figured often in the antebellum debates. George Tucker, for one, followed the Malthusian logic to its conclusion, and predicted the date at which this euthanasia of slavery would occur.[10] Interpreted this way, the viability question has little historical interest. Rather, given the importance of this question in many interpretations of the onset of the Civil War, the viability debate has focused on the years around 1860, asking both what were the planter expectations that year and how accurate were these forecasts.

An analysis of matters of profitability and viability, based upon the examination of price and output data, shall yield certain implications as to the behavior of planters, and also provide some background for the study of their actions and writings, background useful as some indication of the responses of planters as well as of the possible flexibility of the southern economy.

The most recent debate on profitability can probably be traced to the 1958 article of Alfred Conrad and John Meyer, "The Economics of Slavery in the Ante Bellum South."[11] There were, of course, many earlier studies of the question in a similar format. Benjamin Franklin's 1751 analysis of the relative profitability of slavery is clearly in the same framework, and there are no doubt many predecessors to be found in pamphlet literature both on whether slavery should be introduced (as in Georgia) and on the choice of slave vs. indentured vs. free labor. It may be an indication of the effects of the Conrad and Meyer work that what they argue—that slavery was basically a profitable investment to planters—is now regarded by some as so obvious that its demonstration was trivial, and also that it is often overlooked that their results, with emphasis on the sale of offspring to maintain profits in the older areas of the South, were fully compatible with the earlier arguments of John Elliott Cairnes. In some sense the question of profitability, as they examined it, was rather trivial, for slavery could be considered profitable to those willing to pay the price to acquire slaves for feelings of conspicuous consumption or power, and also such conditions would be consistent with some measured degree of price responsiveness. But what Conrad and Meyer really argued was that the price of slaves could be explained without any considerations other than financial returns. At present, the broad consensus seems to be that slavery was profitable to the planters, and in most areas of the South. But, clearly, that is where the study of the slave economy now begins rather than ends.

The issue of viability has, as noted, two aspects. On the first of these, what the planters anticipated in the 1850s, there is some disagreement apparent between those historians relying on what the planters seemed to write and to say, and those examining what the planters were betting their money on for the future. It is clear that the planters, rightly or wrongly, were plowing more money into the system. An example of a people expecting the end of the slave economy (or at least the legal ownership of other humans) can be found in Brazilian planters of the 1870s and 1880s. When a termination became apparent, slave prices collapsed and manumissions increased. In another case, the treatment, during "apprenticeship," of emancipated slaves in the British West Indies, (where a fixed time deadline had been set), apparently became much harsher. The U.S. pattern in the 1850s accords with neither of these.

Of course it is important to know, as Phillips asked, whether the slaveowners were right and, if wrong, how wrong were they. It is now evident that the boom of the 1850s had a very sharp economic impact on the South, and that, unlike most of the nation, the boom didn't end there in 1857. Railroad construction and land sales, for example, held up longer in the South. Given the timing of this boom, it is important to determine whether the oft-quoted rhetoric for expansion was more political than economic in need. It can be argued that the southern political crisis occurred at this time because more people wanted to get into the system where it was already located, and not due to a desire to get out. It is of course possible to ask about the expected developments in the southern economy and the effects upon slave prices, after 1860, under various arguments as to the flexibility of the economy and the usability of land in the settled areas of the South. Gavin Wright concluded that there was a non-sustainable speculative "mania" in the late 1850s, non-sustainable because of the subsequent collapse in cotton demand.[12] Accepting his results for the moment, without questioning his assumptions as to possible long-run productivity trends or to the future flexibility of the southern economy, his most extreme case points to slave prices in 1890 about 35 percent below the 1860 level, an order of loss which would have returned slave prices to the level of the early 1850s. Although this would have been a clear capital loss to purchasers and owners of slaves in this period, it represents a decline less than that which was suffered, and weathered, in the early 1840s within a much shorter space of years.

But, as always, the analysis going into these issues is more interesting and useful than whatever might appear to be the specific answers to these questions. It is important to analyze how planters responded to price incentives, and thus to understand something about this aspect of their motivation. Such a linking is obviously not without its difficulties, but these are difficulties which confront any historical attempt to deal with questions of human behavior and motivation. Given many slaveowning individuals and given the mixed nature of any individual's motivation, it is hard to establish generalizations, although that has not stopped people before. Moreover, it is possible that some behavior patterns are consistent with several different motivations, and disentanglement is not easy. Yet there are a number of aspects of the southern economy which are difficult to explain unless people were doing some calculating and responding to price signals.

Responsiveness to price signals is reflected in various economic patterns in the southern economy. In examining such patterns, there is no desire to show what is obviously not so—that this is all there was to the planters; indeed, it would be equally hard to argue the point for many agreed-upon capitalists of the time. However, such an examination is useful in indicating the flexibility of adjustment in the southern economy, at least within certain clearly defined constraints. The argument to follow, put briefly, is based upon predictions of behavior expected when economic conditions vary, and then a follow-up to see if the outcome accords with these predictions. It is not done independently of looking at what planters said they were doing; rather, it is to see if they did what they said or suggested they would do.

Thus, the profitability calculation, as done initially by Conrad and Meyer, shows the price of slaves responding to the expected value of goods produced by the slaves, in particular to changes in cotton prices and in expected productivity. In this sense and given the supply (more accurately the supply conditions under the assumption of non-regulated fertility), the profitability discussion really concerns how efficiently the data on expected productivity was used in determining slave prices, and whether or not components other than these were needed to explain the movements in the prices of slaves.

The complex structure of slave prices by age, sex, skills, and handicaps indicates that accounting was being made for differences in the productivity of slaves, and that these differences were recognized by planters. Advertisements—which not only listed skills, ages, and handicaps, but also noted the crops grown by the slaves and whether slaves being sold were available in gangs or as family units—as well as the intricate patterns observed in the New Orleans slave market indicate the nature of the detailed calculations made, implicitly or explicitly, by slaveowners.

The movement of slaves, over space, was in the direction of better lands and with a cyclical timing which clearly reflected the economic fluctuations. Moreover, the age pattern of those slaves who were moved, by sale or by relocation with masters, indicates the importance of the price incentives, movement being at those ages, similar to those of the white population, for which the price differentials were large.

Also, the adjustment of the crop-mix to changing relative prices, most particularly the shift in and out of cotton in the nineteenth century, reflected responses to price variables. Thus, the large expansion of cotton output in the 1850s reflected a shift out of corn and other feed crops, and it might be expected that a similar pattern characterized earlier booms. Similarly the movements of slaves in and out of urban areas and, to some extent, industrial pursuits followed a cyclical pattern in which the direction of movement was predictable by looking at the return from cotton.[13] In the 1830s and 1850s when cotton boomed, there was apparently a move out of urban areas, while the 1820s and 1840s, periods of low cotton prices, saw a move into non-agricultural pursuits and industrial uses. While these movements do not fully answer the question posed by Richard Wade, among others, concerning the ultimate optimum level of southern urbanization, they do indicate a flexibility in adjustment within the range of urbanization of the times.

One key indication of planter concern can be seen in the detailed books kept on larger plantation units—records of work routines, of daily amounts of cotton picked and ginned, of purchases, sales, production, slave values, slave births, and slave deaths. It is obvious that not all owners kept such records, and that these usually left much to be desired by current bookkeeping standards. Yet how many other agricultural enterprises kept such records anywhere in the nation? Indeed, with the exception of New England textile mills and large-scale transport units, how many industrial establishments of the North kept such complete accountings? In the pre-anthracite days of pig iron production, the Pennsylvania charcoal iron manufacturers on their plantations kept what must be regarded as extremely inadequate records compared with those found on southern plantations. And it is difficult to look at the journals and periodicals read by southern planters, with their discussions of agricultural methods and arguments for diversification, without sensing that these men were not averse to considerations of increased efficiency and effectiveness within the agricultural economy. While there may have been a failure on the part of southerners to fully follow up on these, it is useful to regard these discussions as attempts at economic innovation rather than as acknowledgments of economic distress.

These remarks about economic flexibility and economic adjustment within a predominantly agricultural economy are suggestive of patterns of behavior within the South which may seem rather unsurprising by now. Yet I think their repetition, besides casting light on the southern plantation system, makes clearer certain aspects of the economic debate. The search for better techniques and methods of organizing labor need not be regarded as a sign of failure. The drive for efficient labor organization and control (whether it meant channeling African work rhythms which happened to be appropriate for an agricultural work year, or else using other forms of externally or internally imposed discipline) was a central part of the plantation system. And the uses of positive incentives and rewards to go with the negative incentives of whippings and threats were important concerns of these landholding, slaveowning planters. In fact, planters focused much attention on the avoidance of the principal difficulty which all classical economists found with slave labor—the presumed lack of incentives (other than fear) in the absence of a system of wage payments and hirings and firings. There were obvious differences between slave and free labor markets in the forms of control. Many classical writers felt that it was the latter market which provided a more complete set of incentives, that being one of the presumed advantages of free labor. In addition to the obvious positive motivations of income and property, commented David Hume, "the fear of punishment will never draw so much labour from a slave, as the dread of being turned off and not getting another service, will from a freeman." [14] After all, those controls most important to establish and regulate a system are not necessarily the only ones which will be found useful or productive on a day-to-day or continuing basis once the system is imposed. Thus, a role for incentives—such as cash, time off, occupational advancement, and even intergenerational transfers of status—as well as the attempt to obtain similar ends by the use of fear and threat were all measures intended to overcome the problem which the classical economists pointed to. The incentives, both negative and positive, did often seem to work, as higher wages and firings did at times for free workers, suggesting that there was some acceptance by slaves of the available opportunities, for whatever reason.

There are further important distinctions to note between free and slave labor systems. The oft-used concept of paternalism has been seen by some to suggest a conflict with a role played by economic goals, a conflict which now seems less stressed. This permits us to better understand those aspects of a paternalism which clearly distinguish slave systems from free labor systems, as well as to comprehend the force of certain constraints upon the strict pursuit of economic goals. As noted, there need be no overriding conflict between paternal attitudes and the desire to make money. Indeed, the characteristics which some have associated with paternalism—good care (which perhaps does not provide the basis for the significant differences discussed) and personal involvement—seem to have been seen by planters as a way to higher profits as well (an equation frequently carried over into the new factory system). What was different was, of course, the extent of control over all aspects of life of the worker, and the close and continuous contact between master and slave, with the important psychological and social impacts on both. All that is noted here is that the sometimes proclaimed conflict between paternalistic attitudes and a response to economic incentives is, for some issues, an artificial and unnecessary one. Some seem to go full circle and try to account for paternalistic attitudes developing in the United States as due not only to technology (the relatively small size of units) or climate (the relative absence of absentee management), but also to the economic pressures of the closing of the slave trade in the Revolutionary War and, finally, legally in 1808. However, the fact that the demographic pattern which was presumably sought by those actions had preceded these dates by at least a century leaves the question of causation and timing still worthy of more study.

The stress on the contribution of an economic motivation in planter behavior is obviously neither new nor, perhaps, worth discussing at such length. For example, when Stanley Elkins described the harshness of the slave system in the United States as uniquely dehumanizing, he attributed it to the "dynamics of unopposed capitalism." And, when Richard Sutch resurrected and expanded upon the perhaps previously buried notion of "slave-breeding," it was with this motive in mind.[15] Infants were worth a positive price, and therefore interference with slave sex lives was, Sutch argues, to be expected. Similarly the arguments (more familiar perhaps in the West Indies but which occasionally have surfaced in the United States) of working slaves to death within a short span of years were based on the same presumed motivation. What seems different in the recent discussion—different but not new since it has an equally long history, not only among defenders of slavery—is the suggestion that, properly considered, the economic goals of the planter may have led to behavior among slaveowners (and slaves) which provided for more favorable treatment and controls than would appear from the earlier discussion of the results of the economic motive. Many of these earlier arguments as to the harsh outcome of the economic motive posit an extremely short operating horizon for owners, and the behavior postulated might make some sense in that event. Yet once we recognize that the concern was for profits over a longer time period, and this concern was justified by the long-term persistence of the slave economy, much more attention need be paid to the morale and interests of the slave labor force. Concern with adequacy of diet, nutrition, and health care is part of developing a productive labor force and can be economically justified, not only by looking at the value of slaves as reflected in their prices, but also by considering the reactions of other slaves to what they see. Of course, it is true that when these aspects of good treatment are found they can be explained as part of the profit-making goals of planters and not a reflection of their humaneness. But this would be no surprise to any reader of Adam Smith nor to the rising industrialists, then and now. This behavior would reflect no moral grandeur, but, as suggested by Smith, might be a perhaps unexpected byproduct of greed.

Another case where planter interests deserve more careful analysis relates to the uniquely high fertility among the American slave population. It was often suggested in the past that such high fertility could not have represented a human reaction to slavery and, therefore, there must have been some direct interference with the lives of slaves to generate this many children. Fitted into the twentieth-century debates about the black family, it became possible to trace a line from this presumed interference to later family instability. And since slave infants had positive values at birth, clearly offspring were welcomed by owners. Yet the nature of the interference postulated for owners was often vague. Indeed, it was often suggested by the slaveowners that the best way to increase reproduction was via the encouragement of stable families, an encouragement of that arrangement which (at least until several years ago) was considered to be the most desirable but presumably precluded by slavery. Perhaps this could be called interference, but certainly not of the form usually discussed. And we must recognize from the postemancipation attitudes of the black southern population in regard to family life that the magnitude, whatever it may have been, of breakups imposed by slave sales was not sufficient to disrupt these developments. The "space" allowed slaves in several areas of life, such as family, could follow from the willingness of masters, in awareness of their interests, to restrict certain forms of interference with slave life. This would provide conditions in which the various recently discussed aspects of slave society could develop, even while it represented a situation in which masters did not themselves dictate the slave patterns of behavior. The point in Elkins' concentration camp image is that a slaveowner may have had controls over many aspects of the lives of the slaves if he wished to push issues to the limit. The question is whether this was desirable to the owner, for economic or for other reasons. It now seems clear that this extreme control was not attempted often, leaving room for slaves to develop patterns of behavior combining the African past and the American present. And, of course, this meant also that the planter was not in absolute control, but found himself molded somewhat by the enslaved.

Such planter responses to economic incentives point to expected patterns of behavior which, of course, were not always realized, both because of extenuating factors which might at times affect individuals, and because there were no doubt individuals to whom other motives were quite important. At times there was a lack of ability—financial, psychological, or otherwise—to obtain even limited achievement of desired ends. One is always hesitant about attempts at generalization, particularly for such large aggregates as slaveholders and slaves, but such attempts are not unique to recent scholars. The effort to find general patterns is crucial in describing the framework in which such behavior and its effects upon the enslavers and the enslaved can be understood. And, more broadly, in trying to describe the operations of a system to explain its impact, we can do more than point to what was legally possible or what may have occurred a limited number of times— points central, of course, to the moral condemnation of the existing institution. The relationship between occurrences and attitudes is a frequently discussed aspect of the historical debate. Is it not possible that the psychological impacts on the enslaved would differ if, for example, all slaves were whipped frequently or "only" some fraction, or if 90 percent as opposed to 15 percent of families were broken by sale, or if 50 percent suffered nutritional inadequacy as opposed to 5 percent?[16] A psychological impact will follow limited occurrence, or even the threat in the absence of occurrences, but this does not tell us that the impact will not vary with the frequency observed. In a serious endeavor to understand the enslaved, these are important questions.

Several of the recent works on slavery and the events occurring immediately after emancipation and during Reconstruction imply a certain pattern of master and slave behavior, a pattern in which recognition of the constraints imposed by long-run profit-seeking provides a useful framework in which this behavior can be understood. But what does this have to do with discussions about whether the southern economy was capitalistic as opposed to non-capitalistic, acapitalistic, precapitalistic, or anticapitalistic, or non-bourgeois, abourgeois, prebourgeois, or antibourgeois? Perhaps very little for certain definitions of these crucial concepts. Before turning to such broader themes, it is useful to remember that, whatever term might be applied to the South, it did not preclude a response to economic incentives within that predominantly agricultural structure. What is at issue is the explanation for the economic structure of the South. Why was there less manufacturing industry in the South than elsewhere in the United States? This is a question obviously important to answer, but, again, not one which denies a response to economic incentives within the existing economic and political system.

IV

Perhaps the most crucial, and certainly the most interesting, of the earlier debates on slave economies did not really question these aspects of private behavior and motivation. Rather, the argument accepted that while planters might be seeking (and making) profits, the net outcome of the slavery system would be to generate a lower income for the particular geographic area than would have occurred in the existence of another form of labor organization. Before discussing what we know (or think we do) about the southern economy, note the information this basic comparison requires—such as analysis of the possible differences in settlement patterns (how many people? how close together?) as well as in crop patterns (what will be grown and on what size units?)—before a meaningful discussion can be undertaken.

Three related questions will be discussed here: (1) the rate of growth of the southern economy and the level and distribution of its income and wealth, (2) the efficiency of economic production within the system, and (3) the specific economic structure of the southern economy. Discussion of these questions are important not only for understanding the nature of the slave economy, but also in providing a background for the analysis of economic patterns in the postbellum South. These are, of course, issues which have been widely debated in recent times. What must seem the same points have been gone over innumerable times without there being any apparent agreement on specific issues of interpretation. Given this I shall touch on some points rather briefly, not because they are considered unimportant but because we have been through much of this before and are still arguing about what it means.

In terms of economic growth, total and per capita, the South was growing rapidly in the last antebellum decades, and, based on some rather crude estimates, probably for the entire nineteenth century.[17] The level of per capita income in 1860 was high by most standards, while the level of output per capita (and per worker) fell after the Civil War in a quite dramatic fashion. The 1870 per capita agricultural output in the five major cotton-producing states was 60 percent of that of 1859, and even in 1880 it was only 70 percent of the antebellum level.[18] In the antebellum period there were marked differences in levels and rates of growth among the subregions of the South, and, as frequently noted, more of the southern growth was due to interregional shifts than in the North.

The issue, perhaps, is not whether southern income levels and their growth rates were high, but rather whether they could have been higher and whether they could have been sustained. Growth in this period was related to the expansion of world cotton demand, as in the previous century it was influenced by the tobacco markets in Europe. An inability for antebellum growth to continue has been argued from both demand and supply sides. Gavin Wright has recently provided econometric estimates suggesting a fall in the growth of demand for American cotton, while Charles Ramsdell earlier had presented two supply arguments, pointing to the decline of the southern economy.[19] One, the natural limits, followed from Cairnes; Ramsdell argued that supply would not be able to grow rapidly. The second argument claimed, not quite consistently, that railroads into Texas would increase supply so rapidly that a sharp price fall would occur. Some disentangling of these issues is useful, particularly since Wright's estimates of the demand for cotton show it to be sufficiently inelastic to pose some paradoxical results concerning the effects of more land and more slaves on southern wealth. And although the demand may have been unique and perhaps non-sustainable, this was perhaps no more so than in England and other areas dependent on what may in retrospect appear as unique configurations. Growth in the South had a rather long history by the standards of most economies. Thus, concentration on the various expected long-run effects after 1860 could lead to a misreading of the politics and society of the antebellum world.

On the issue of income and wealth distribution, recent works on the manuscript censuses dealing with wealth have managed to provide indications helpful to the arguments on all sides. For while there was more inequality of wealth among whites in rural areas of the South than in rural areas of the North, because of the greater urban concentrations in the latter and the greater inequalities in wealth there, the distribution of wealth among white southerners did not differ from that in the North, and was no doubt more equal than in the major European areas.[20] These distribution estimates suggest the need for a new look at the yeoman and the "poor whites" of the South to see exactly how and why they were affected, both economically and politically. The issue of wealth distribution is important not only as an indication of how the benefits of growth were shared in the South, but also because the arguments about southern markets question whether this distribution was sufficiently unequal to make consumption and savings patterns incompatible with economic growth. For this reason, data on the magnitude and composition of imported manufactured goods would provide some useful information on market potential.

On another familiar economic issue, some consensus has developed from recent work, although, as in the results of the studies of wealth distributions, the data can be used by all sides of the debate. It had previously been argued that the South needed to import foods, and that this was an indication of its inefficient production. However, recent studies of trade patterns indicate that the South was relatively self-sufficient in food production.[21] But then there is the contention that this self-sufficiency precluded the development of internal markets and of small-scale processing which could have spurred economic growth in the future, thus making the South's adjustment in the postbellum period difficult.

One of the most discussed of all issues in the economics of slavery, perhaps because it might seem the easiest comparison to make, is that of the relative efficiency of slave vs. free labor. In many cases the argument was made purely on the basis of incentives, and as David Brion Davis and Eric Foner have pointed out, became quite central to the arguments in Britain and in the North concerning the development of the free labor market.[22] The earlier argument, based upon incentives, later became mixed with more racist issues concerning the relative abilities of different races; with both arguments pointing in the same direction, they became mutually reinforcing.

As generally worded, the efficiency comparison poses a question which seemingly can be answered with a fairly straightforward economic procedure. There have been many studies to determine for which economy or in which time period a higher output could be obtained from given amounts of inputs of land, labor, and capital. For comparisons over time this procedure has been used by economists for the past thirty years, applied to situations in which there have been considerable differences in output mix. More recently there have been a number of studies providing international productivity comparisons among nations. While the initial interest was in U.S.–U.S.S.R. comparisons, there have also been, among others, comparisons of the United States with Western Europe and with Latin America. Although these comparisons have their difficulties, the method provides extremely useful comparative information with which to begin further detailed analysis of the factors behind any measured difference.

When Robert Fogel and I first measured the total factor productivity of the southern economy, in an article first published in 1971, we felt that this economist's tool provided a means of studying a question which had been long posed. We thought that since the question had long been asked in terms of outputs for certain inputs, with a recognition of the different output mixes in the regions, the application seemed straightforward.[23] As we reported then, and three years later on the basis of more detailed examinations of individual farms made possible by the extensive sampling undertaken in census manuscripts for 1860 by William Parker and Robert Gallman, it appeared that it was the South and not the North which obtained more output (physical outputs valued at a common set of price) from its inputs of land, labor, and capital.[24] Further, within the South measured efficiency was highest on the larger units using slave labor. This interesting measure helped us understand and put in perspective various aspects of planter and slave behavior. While the distinction between high measured efficiency in producing output and welfare to members of society was well known, we felt that this was an answer to a traditional question, which similarly was about measured output and not optimum welfare.

This conclusion has attracted some discussion, and this is not the

place to enter either defense or critical extension of the procedures. Rather, I wish here only to note two aspects of this discussion which I think have useful implications for the study of southern society. It has been argued that the differences in crop-mixes,
among other reasons, make these comparisons worthless or impossible. Also, some point to the atypicality of 1860 as imposing an
artificially favorable outcome in such a comparison for the southern states.

Clearly the crop-mix issue poses problems, as do the differences
in climate, land quality, and natural resources. I presume that if
we took all the methodological proscriptions seriously, whether as
economists or historians, we would all have retired years ago.
None of us do, but rather try to make as much sense of imperfect
procedures as we can. If we did take the methodological proscriptions about incomparability seriously we would, of course, find not
only that the procedures can't tell us that the South was more
efficient than the North, but also that there is no way to show that
the North was more efficient than the South. In other words, the
entire debate would have been about a non-question which can't
be pursued, and a lot of people have therefore been wasting much
time. Clearly the attempts to compare North and South—no
matter how dissimilar crop-mix, climate, and land—have a long
history which involves assuming the two regions fully comparable
in economic potential. The frequency of North–South comparisons when arguing for southern backwardness would make no
sense without that assumption. Moreover, while the results might
be influenced by the particular configuration of world demand and
southern natural resources, if the demand for cotton disappeared
and no resources could be transferred elsewhere, measured efficiency could be low. It remains possible that, if labor and other
inputs were used inefficiently or if the southern planters did not
adjust to take advantage of their best agricultural alternative, the
measure could provide the expected greater northern efficiency.
Indeed, this suggests a way to see the extent to which the particu-

lar results are sensitive to the level of cotton demand in any given year. Various estimates of the demand for cotton both prior and subsequent to 1860 have been presented. Let us first assume a demand curve for cotton in 1860, which in the extreme case falls completely away after resources were devoted to cotton production. Since cotton was less than 29 percent of southern output, this price of zero, no matter how large the crop, would just about leave the South relatively as efficient as the North, accepting the other assumptions of our adjusted index.[25] If we use the unadjusted index—ignoring the problem of land valuation by using physical acreage (and thus biasing the result against the South by not separating improved from unimproved acres)—and the cotton output implied by Gavin Wright's long-run supply and demand curves, the same conclusion of higher relative efficiency for the South remains. These comparisons indicate that, once the suggested calculations are performed, the results for 1860 (and earlier years) are not dependent solely on the particular configuration of cotton demand in that year.

Therefore, the high level of cotton demand is neither necessary nor sufficient to yield any specific conclusions as to relative efficiency. And while the South might have had favorable land for cotton, its land was of rather poor quality and its climate and soil ill-suited to take full advantage of rising demands for wheat and livestock production.[26] Climatic conditions in the South were not ideal for textile production at that time, and the region lacked such natural resources as iron and coal necessary for industrial development. Southern harbors were also inadequate compared with those of the North. Obviously, all natural advantages were not on the southern side.

Moreover, the fact that the same climate would occur for all farms in the South permits a comparison of large and small farms within that area to determine how the productive efficiency varied with size. The results suggest greater measured efficiency on large-scale units. It was these farms which were concentrated in the production of cotton relative to other crops (although they were often self-sufficient in food production), these farms which had higher measured output for given inputs of land, labor, and capital. A specialization away from cotton on smaller units is difficult to understand, unless there were benefits to larger scale or unless family farmers either preferred more leisure (thus growing less cotton after their food requirements were met) or willingly paid a high price in foregone income and time to grow their own food.[27] The latter are, of course, possibilities and it would be useful to determine which of these courses was chosen by southern whites. (The second of these would be consistent with economies of scale, the former not). More detailed information on the allocation of time by planters and farmers, on all size farms, would not only help resolve these issues but also yield insight into the motivation and behavior of the free white farmer of the South.

It is quite true that 1860 was an excellent year for cotton. The output, in particular, was unusually high, and the price also remained high, implying a large growth in cotton demand. But this growth in cotton output was not achieved at zero cost in resources to the southern economy. There was markedly slow growth in the output of corn and sweet potatoes, and for most other commodities growth was slower than in the North.[28] The net effect of this shift can be seen in looking at the breakdown of the Towne–Rasmussen agricultural series for these census years. While cotton output increased by nearly 90 percent in the USDA-based estimates (by 118 percent using census data), the share of cotton revenue in southern agricultural output increased by less than 3 percentage points, from 26 percent to 28.4 percent.[29] Indeed for the decade, the value of northern agricultural income grew more rapidly than did southern, as did northern inputs of labor, acres, and implements. Thus, a similar calculation of the unadjusted index for 1850, a year when cotton output was below that predicted by Wright's equation, yields the same result as does our 1860 calculation, a higher measured southern efficiency, and of roughly the same magnitude. Moreover, in using the adjusted measures, it is probable that the 1850 southern efficiency advantage would look higher than it does in 1860, since there was a larger increase in southern than northern land values in the decade, perhaps capturing some of the effects of the cotton boom. While it is difficult to use the census data for earlier years, the differences for 1840 in output per worker (when cotton was less than one-fifth of southern output) are comparable with these later results.[30] Whatever may have happened past 1860, a pattern of higher measured efficiency can be found in preceding years for the South. If it is desired to argue that this was unique to the years after 1840, there is still presumably a need to explain the large growth in relative southern efficiency in the first half of the nineteenth century.

The economies of scale and the participation rate effects, the former explaining higher measured efficiency and the latter pointing to a higher measured output in the South under slavery, can both help explain much of the postbellum income decline in the South. It was, in part, not the natural legacy of a slave economy, but rather a return to the level expected in a free labor society. The reduction in labor force participation rates explains part, but only part, of this decline. Some of that which remains may be due to the movement to smaller scale units which precluded taking advantage of economies of scale. Here, again, more detailed study, this time of ex-slave work routines (in contrast with those of white farmers) would be helpful in analyzing the nature of the slave society and its customs.

These efficiency calculations do cast light on the southern economy and provide a useful framework for analysis, whatever the result or outcome of various refinements and adjustments might be. They suggest that ending the slave system was not costless to consumers, but that is perhaps not a very surprising outcome. Mainly these calculations point to certain economic advantages of the slave form of labor organization. Of course, this depended upon a certain demand pattern to permit the taking of the benefits of economies of scale, but were there not similar "unique" configurations for the textile industry or the iron industry? The southern planters were able to organize their labor force to take advantage of these demand and technological patterns, in the same way as businessmen in the North were able to combine technology and labor in developing factories. And the planters were able to accomplish this for quite long periods of time with rather limited expenditures on means of controlling the black population. The southerners solved the problem of controlling a labor force in productive ways, whether this meant the creation of new work routines by slaves or the channeling of their earlier work routines, and owners were able to use skilled labor to organize and produce on farms and in cities with a limited degree of regulation. The particular mix of fear and internalization of the methods of the system permitting this control at relatively low financial cost has long been, and continues to be, in dispute. Workers may have been unhappy and disruptive. Yet this was not sufficient to eliminate the large financial payoffs to their owners. That the system of threat, reward, coercion, and paternalism worked seems clear. Whether it was the fear imposed, the patterns resulting from paternalistic dependence, or the fact that adopted patterns useful in a certain type of agriculture were not adaptable to others, which imposed higher long-run costs on the enslaved is, as always, a fascinating question. Moreover, these problems of labor control, discipline, and internalization of effort were not unique to slavery, as David Brion Davis' discussion relating to the creation of the English industrial labor force has demonstrated. In chapters which might bring a hearty nod of approval from George Fitzhugh, Davis has carefully examined the similar problems, handled with perhaps greater long-run success, of English factory owners. And we know that the northern labor force posed similar difficulties throughout the century.

It will be noted that I have not yet dealt with the question of why the economic structure of the South differed from that of the

North, and the issues of the costs this imposed and the time at which costs did or could have occurred. I wish only to comment that it is not enough to argue that this inefficiency, if we call it that, occurred. Rather, as a guide to the political and social history of the South, it is necessary to more adequately deal with the causes of this pattern. An economist might suggest this specialization, providing a high income to slave society, was due to the comparative advantage of growing a commodity in high demand (at least until 1860), but that might seem too easy an answer as well as one seeming to avoid the possible legacies for postbellum adjustment. More to the point, if we allow for some private rationality of entrepreneurs and planters, there is the difficulty of explaining whether the failure to shift to industry can be attributed to their perception of either supply or demand forces. Was this failure due to a "limited market size," or to an unwillingness, for purposes of control, to permit concentrations of slaves in more urban and industrial areas? Was it due to the planters' lack of interest in the money and power to be obtained from an alternative way of life, or, given that others might have been willing to fill this vacuum, the fear that they might lose political control if such attempts were permitted? In other words, was this presumed ability to preclude urban-industrial development the result of sharp political conflict or did it flow smoothly out of the hegemony imposed by planters? As might be anticipated, I am skeptical about many of the points customarily made in arguments about causes and costs to the southern economy. There are many different adjustments made by economies specializing in export production when market conditions shift (ranging from Australia and New Zealand, on one hand, through South Africa, and Argentina, to Latin America), and for the important questions of interest to political and social historians it is not enough to point to a correlation between slavery and lack of industry. Rather, given the many different explanations with their various implications for all aspects of southern behavior, it remains of interest to try to analyze the role of these factors in creating this presumed contrast between private and social efficiency for the southern economy.

V

It is clear that I have at times ranged quite far afield from the strictly economic issues. From measures of the specifics of the outputs produced by slaves and of the details of the calculation of regional income statistics to attempts to depict the nature of southern society and the life conditions and modes of behavior adopted by the enslaved may seem a rather long and disconnected leap. Yet, of course, this wider flow from narrow economics to broader issues of society and culture has always characterized the debate on the slave economy, and no doubt may explain the continued interest and debate about this particular aspect of the peculiar labor institution of the antebellum South. The study of the economic issues may not tell us all we wish to know about the South, but it is difficult to find a more important starting point for our understanding of slavery, and what it meant to all southerners, black as well as white.

Slavery—The White Man's Burden

WILLIAM K. SCARBOROUGH

As we enter the bicentennial year, it is altogether fitting that we in the historical profession should focus our attention upon the institution of Negro slavery. In many respects the blight of slavery constitutes one of the most lamentable chapters in the history of the American republic. For, more than any other institution in the two hundred years of our existence as a nation, it has served to divide our people and to tarnish the lofty principles upon which this country was founded. Indeed, even now the legacy of slavery continues to engender strife and bitterness.

Yet, there is another side to the ledger. Despite the debilitating influence of slavery—especially upon blacks—the plantation society of the Old South was not without its virtues. The export trade in southern staples played a vital role in the development of commerce and industry, not only in the United States but throughout the Western world. Moreover, the civilization of which slavery was an integral part spawned a remarkable galaxy of political leaders who, in large measure, laid the foundations of our democratic republic. It would be difficult to imagine the path

The author wishes to express his gratitude to the National Endowment for the Humanities for a grant, awarded during the summer of 1967, to promote research at the Louisiana State University Department of Archives for a forthcoming monograph on "Planter Dynasties of the Old South." Some material obtained during that summer residency in Baton Rouge has been incorporated in this paper.

which this nation would have traveled without the services of such slaveholders as George Mason, George Washington, Thomas Jefferson, James Madison, John Marshall, and Andrew Jackson—to name but a few of the most obvious. Subsequent generations, both white and black, have benefited from the monumental contributions which these men rendered to the American political system.

Historians have long been fascinated by the subject of slavery. It is doubtful whether any other facet of the American experience has been studied more assiduously nor claimed more of their time and talents. Apart from its manifest historical significance, there are several reasons for this perennial interest. To some scholars, especially non-southerners, it seems to have an almost exotic attraction, representing a society and culture totally alien to their own. To others it is seen as a vehicle by which to better understand and seek solutions to contemporary problems. There can be little doubt that much of the recent interest in slavery was sparked by the civil rights revolution, which induced blacks to embark upon the quest for a separate identity and caused many whites to seek a convenient scapegoat by which to expiate the guilt produced by more than three centuries of discrimination against black Americans.[1]

Whatever the cause, the last two decades have witnessed the publication of a plethora of books and articles relating to the slave experience in America. Almost without exception, these writings have been of uncommonly high quality. Especially significant have been the efforts to eradicate racism from a depiction of the slave South and to view the institution of slavery from the perspective of those who endured its iniquities. To this end new sources, such as the autobiographies of former slaves and the extensive slave narrative collection, have been employed skillfully and judiciously by such scholars as John W. Blassingame and Eugene D. Genovese. New techniques, such as the psychoanalytical approach pioneered by Stanley M. Elkins and the sophisticated methodology of the cliometricians, have been utilized with checkered success. Others have opted for new approaches, of which one of the most productive has been the comparative study of different slave societies. Thus, from Kenneth M. Stampp's superb study, which appeared in 1956, to the towering works of Robert Fogel and Stanley Engerman, Genovese, and David B. Davis within the past year, each in its own way has served to enhance our understanding of that unique phenomenon which was the Old South.

However, despite the many advances, recent studies of slavery are not without their deficiencies. Understandably influenced by the civil rights crusade, some scholars, especially those writing in the 1950s, have tended to portray the material conditions of slave life too harshly. More recent writers, while conceding that the system was marked by a high degree of paternalism, seem constrained to view all acts of benevolence as either self-serving or motivated solely by considerations of economics or social control. Thus, although much progress has been made in clarifying the attitudes and personality types of the slaves, that progress has been at the expense of distorting the character and motivations of the masters. Consequently, I shall here attempt to view the institution of slavery from the perspective of the slaveholding class, especially the great planters, and in the process to respond to certain interpretations propounded in recent years by scholars of the slave South.

I hope that my subsequent remarks will not be misconstrued as constituting a defense of slavery or as betraying an insensitivity to the very real sufferings of black people under slavery. In emphasizing the paternalistic character of southern slavery, I do not mean to minimize the inherent inhumanity and brutality of depriving any individual of his personal freedom and his dignity as a human being. That, of course, is an inescapable and central feature of every slave system, and in the Old South it was compounded by the added ingredient of racism.

Having admitted this, however, I think it is imperative to remember that slavery, in one form or another, had been a part of the human experience in the Western world since the beginning of recorded history. Antebellum southerners did not originate the institution of chattel slavery. Instead, they drifted into it, adopting it gradually, by custom—not step-by-step as a matter of deliberate choice, as Professor Stampp has argued.[2] Moreover, they were aided and abetted in its establishment by European merchants, Yankee slavetraders, and tribal chieftains in Africa. By the nineteenth century most white southerners had come to regard it as the foundation-stone of their socioeconomic system, as the right institution in the right place at the right time. However much we may deplore that judgment, we should not allow the moral outrage engendered by twentieth-century moral and ethical standards to color our interpretation of one of the most remarkable classes in American history, the planters of the slave South.

As one peruses the diaries, correspondence, and business records of the large slaveholders, it is difficult not to be impressed with the breadth of their knowledge, with their intellectual curiosity and versatility. Educated in the finest universities of Europe and America, trained to leadership, inculcated with the social graces, they scarcely conformed to the image of "barbarians" projected by James Russell Lowell and other abolitionist critics. In this age of cultural mediocrity, one can only marvel at an Edmund Ruffin, who, before he was eleven years old, had read all of Shakespeare's plays.[3] Nor was Ruffin unique among his class in this respect. If the planters made few original contributions to the arts, they at least appreciated their worth and cultivated them assiduously. But it was in the fields of statecraft and agriculture that they particularly excelled, and it is to the latter that we must now turn our attention.

Notwithstanding fervid protestations to the contrary by Professor Genovese, the landed proprietors of the Old South were tough-minded businessmen—capitalists in every sense of the word. The profit motive is a dominant theme in the personal correspondence and business papers of virtually every planter who has left a record of his operations. They were constantly expanding their enterprises and seeking new investment opportunities, many of which were outside the agricultural sector. It may well be true that few lower-class whites were imbued with bourgeois ideals, but that does not negate the existence of such ideals among members of the planter and merchant classes. Morton Rothstein has suggested that the economic structure of the Old South can best be understood by viewing it as a "dual economy," in which slaves and poor whites constituted the traditional sector while yeoman farmers, artisans, planters, and the business and professional classes comprised the dominant bourgeois-oriented group.[4] This seems to me to be a sound approach.

Few Americans of the nineteenth century exhibited more pronounced bourgeois characteristics than Dr. Stephen Duncan of Natchez and Duncan F. Kenner of Louisiana. A native of Carlisle, Pennsylvania, Duncan settled in Mississippi shortly before the War of 1812 and soon established a plantation empire based on cotton and sugar. During the 1850s, he was the largest resident slaveowner in Mississippi, with holdings in excess of 1,000, and his plantations were yielding annual net returns of more than $150,000. He invested much of this surplus capital in northern railroad securities and public lands in the Midwest. An uncompromising foe of secession and the Confederacy, Duncan abandoned his palatial Natchez residence in the spring of 1863 and fled to New York City. There he gained some solace from an inventory of his estate which revealed total assets of $1,060,000 exclusive of plantations and slaves.[5] Kenner, one of the most successful sugar planters in Louisiana both before and after the Civil War, had interests in many other slices of the economic pie. At his death in 1887 he owned a large quantity of stocks and bonds, an entire block of buildings on Carondelet Street in New Orleans, and was president of the New Orleans Gas Light Company, two oil companies, the Louisiana Cotton Manufacturing Company, and the Louisiana Sulphur and Mining Company.[6]

Countless other examples could be cited. Two of the leading sugar planters, Maunsel White and John Burnside, both immigrants from Northern Ireland, made their initial fortunes in the mercantile business in New Orleans. Are we to infer that they suddenly abandoned their bourgeois principles when they entered the agricultural sector? Or what of the other Natchez nabobs—men like William J. Minor, Levin R. Marshall, William Newton Mercer—all of whom were heavily involved in banking, real estate, and foreign investments.[7] If such men as these were not capitalists, then perhaps that term requires redefinition.

One final point should be made. When southern writers attacked the evils of northern capitalism—wage slavery, as they called it—they did so, not out of any ideological aversion to the market-oriented, profit-motivated economic system of which they were very much a part, but as a means of defending their peculiar labor system of chattel slavery. Economics, like the Bible, ethnology, history, and natural law, simply became another weapon in the proslavery arsenal. And the thrust of their argument was that the wage slaves of the North fared worse in a material sense than the chattel slaves of the South because the former system lacked the key ingredient of paternalism, which was in fact a central feature of southern slavery.

As Fogel and Engerman have observed, there is no inherent conflict between capitalism and paternalism; the two are not mutually exclusive.[8] One has only to look to the paternalistic mill villages of the New South, or to George Pullman's model town in Illinois, or even to such modern corporations as Kodak, to discover examples of capitalistic enterprises which practiced paternalism. There is no doubt that the planter-capitalists of the Old South exhibited toward their black laborers a unique form of paternalism, which operated to mitigate in some degree the evils which are inherent in any slave system. In his latest book,[9] Professor Genovese has elucidated with remarkable perception the paternalistic relationship which bound together masters and slaves in the Old South. My principal quarrel with his interpretation lies in his characterization of the planters, especially in his distressing propensity to assign to them only base and ignoble motives for acts of genuine benevolence.

This is not to say, of course, that all slaveholders were actuated by honorable motives. The personality types of the masters were as varied as those of the slaves, delineated so brilliantly by Professor Blassingame in his recent book,[10] or of mankind generally. There were sadistic masters as well as benevolent ones. But just as the slaves exhibited certain common traits, so too did those who governed them. It is my contention that the class as a whole, especially at the highest level, was permeated by a sense of honor, noblesse oblige, chivalry, justice, Christian compassion; in a word, the typical planter was a gentleman, a term which is ubiquitous in the correspondence of the period. It was this quality, for example, that induced Edmund Ruffin to intercede with the governor of Virginia in behalf of a slave in his county who had been wrongfully implicated in the Nat Turner conspiracy. He wrote and circulated a petition, which he then carried personally to Richmond, in a vain effort to procure a pardon for the accused Negro. As a consequence, he incurred "much odium" from his neighbors and was threatened with "personal violence."[11] I submit that there was nothing "self-serving" about this act or others of similar character.

In their recent works, Genovese and Blassingame quite correctly emphasize the vital role of religion in promoting self-respect among blacks, thus enabling them to preserve their emotional health and to resist the dehumanizing aspects of slavery. Yet they seem oblivious to any benign or ameliorative influence which that same force may have exerted upon members of the slaveholding class. The fact is, of course, that Christianity was a powerful factor in the lives of most antebellum southerners, both black and white. Although most southern whites saw no inherent incompatibility between Christian doctrine and the ownership of slaves, their diaries and letters reveal that many of them were devoutly religious and committed sincerely to the basic tenets of Christianity, at least as they understood them. Thus, it was a combination of Christian compassion and economic interest which produced near-unanimous agreement among planters that the welfare of their slaves was the paramount consideration. As one Mississippi slaveholder observed, no subject demanded more careful attention by the master than the proper treatment of his slaves, "by whose labor he lives, and for whose happiness and conduct he is responsible in the eyes of God."[12]

In many respects the relationship between master and slave was analogous to that between a father and his children, as, indeed, the word "paternalism" implies. This view was expressed explicitly by Maunsel White when he wrote, "we view our Slaves almost in the same light we do our Children."[13] The typical planter treated his slaves with justice, humanity, and compassion; in return, he expected—indeed, demanded—obedience, loyalty, and good deportment. Just as the father was omnipotent in his own household, so too was the proprietor omnipotent within the realm of the plantation. He had great power—indeed, the power of life and death over his black wards—but in most cases he exercised that power responsibly. For those not naturally disposed to govern in such a manner, peer pressure was an important factor in enforcing conformity to the norm. Those who earned the reputation of being cruel masters usually incurred the odium of their neighbors and suffered social ostracism.

Let us turn now to a more specific consideration of the treatment accorded slaves on southern plantations. One of the most unfortunate consequences of the continuing onslaught upon *Time on the Cross* is the tendency to reject summarily virtually all of the major interpretations advanced in that work.[14] While holding serious reservations about the methodological techniques employed by Fogel and Engerman, as well as about a number of their conclusions, I am persuaded that they were essentially correct in their depiction of the material conditions of slave life. There is abundant evidence from the traditional sources to sustain the position that benevolent paternalism was practiced widely, if not universally, in the slave South; that blacks were treated pretty well as slaves, if not as human beings.

To make my case as persuasive as possible, I have drawn almost exclusively upon the records of large plantations and especially upon data relating to the operation of Louisiana sugar plantations, where, presumably, conditions were worse than anywhere else. Because of the closer personal relationship between master and slave on small farms, it is generally conceded that blacks fared better on those units than on large plantations where they usually labored under the direct supervision of a white overseer. Likewise, there is common agreement that slaves were driven more relentlessly on sugar estates, especially during the rolling season, than on other staple-producing plantations. Consequently, the general picture of slave treatment and living conditions which emerges from a perusal of such records should, if anything, exaggerate the harshness of the slave regime.

One of the standard privileges accorded southern slaves was freedom from labor on certain days of the year. Even by modern criteria, the great planters were generous in their allocation of holidays. Sunday was customarily a day of rest except on Louisiana sugar plantations during the grinding season. Even there, some proprietors interrupted the boiling process to give the usual day of rest. Both Valcour Aime and Bishop Leonidas Polk granted Sunday holidays during rolling, and the master of Bayside plantation paid his Negroes for Sunday work during that period.[15] Many planters gave occasional whole or half-holidays on Saturdays. In addition, most masters granted their hands a brief respite at the conclusion of each cycle in the agricultural routine—e.g., at the end of planting, after the crop was laid by, at the conclusion of harvest. Special events, such as slave weddings and funerals, were usually preceded by whole or half-holidays. Similarly, when two

Plaquemines Parish sugar plantations escaped the ravages of a spring crevasse which devastated nearly every other plantation in the vicinity, the servants from both units joined the white population on both sides of the river in a gigantic Thanksgiving barbecue replete with claret and champagne. In the Upper South it was a common practice to give holiday on both Easter Monday and Whit Monday, though both fell during spring planting.[16] But, apart from Christmas, the most universally observed national holiday was the Fourth of July. Not all planters celebrated this holiday, but those who did took their commitment seriously. When the great flood of 1858 forced Maunsel White to work his hands on that date, the proprietor recorded this apology: "people all at Work this day which I Pray god to forgive us for. but it is a work of necessity which keeps us raising Banks to keep out the Waters of the Crevasses now Pouring down upon us." On those occasions when July 4 fell on a Sunday, most masters who normally observed it gave either the preceding or the following day as a holiday.[17]

The most extended slave holiday, of course, was given at Christmas. Normally lasting from three to seven days and highlighted by dancing, trips to town, gifts from the master, and at least one sumptuous repast, it was always a gala occasion for plantation blacks. Typical is the following entry from the plantation diary of John Carmichael Jenkins, a Natchez planter: "Christmas day—we shall not have any work done until beginning of New Year."[18] Jenkins, an especially compassionate master, personally distributed a gift to each of his slaves after the annual tree lighting on Christmas Eve at his Elgin plantation. Such gifts might include molasses, whisky, tobacco, and calico for the adults or toys, candy, and fruit for the children. One writer, who has made an intensive study of the manuscript records of Natchez area planters, found no instance in which Christmas Day was not a holiday, nor any in which slaves did not receive some sort of gift from their owners. Moreover, she determined that the *average* length of the Christmas holiday in that Deep South region was seven days.[19]

Many planters distributed substantial sums of money to their Negroes at Christmas, either as recompense for poultry and garden produce raised by the hands or in lieu of that privilege.[20] Thus, in 1840 Bennet H. Barrow, a master not noted for his benevolence, dispensed $700 to his slave force, which numbered 129.[21] Two years later, caught in the midst of a severe economic depression, he wrote: "Gave the negros as much of Evry thing to eat & *drink* during the Hollidays as they Wanted times so hard no[t] able to give any thing more." Other planters, such as John A. Selden, proprietor of Westover plantation on the James River, customarily gave their people a bountiful provisions allowance each Christmas. In 1861 Selden distributed to his 63 Negroes "350 lbs. of Bacon & Beef—2 bls of superfine flour 1 pint of molasses each, lard &c for their xmas."[22]

Only on Louisiana sugar plantations, where the process of making sugar often extended through Christmas and into the new year, was their no respite for southern slaves during the yuletide season. And there the holiday was simply postponed until the end of rolling. Looking at the South as a whole and taking into account customary holidays, special events, and days on which inclement weather prevented any work, it is fair to say that most slaves received annual holidays amounting in the aggregate to from ten to fourteen days, exclusive of Sundays and partial Saturdays.

It was a standard practice on many plantations to permit slaves to raise poultry and to plant gardens on small plots of ground allocated to each family for that purpose. These privileges served two functions. First, they enabled the hands to supplement their basic fare of pork and corn meal, provided by the master, with such garden produce as peas, sweet potatoes, and pumpkins, as well as poultry and eggs. The effect was to add variety to the slave diet. But second, and perhaps more important, they provided a means by which the slaves could earn spending money with which to purchase coffee, sugar, tobacco products, Christmas presents, and other luxuries. A number of the major planters allowed their slaves to raise corn and hay on these individual plots. They then purchased these slave crops, often disbursing large sums of money for them.[23] For example, in 1847 Valcour Aime paid his Negroes, which numbered just over 200, the startling amount of $1300 for their corn. Similarly, John C. Jenkins and Stephen Duncan regularly expended several hundred dollars each year for products raised by their hands.[24] Such a system clearly served as a positive incentive for the slaves, allowing them a certain measure of personal freedom in purchasing consumer items and enabling black males to resist the emasculation process by providing more adequately for their families.

A few of the more benevolent planters developed sophisticated variations of the incentive system described above. The Bringier family of Louisiana operated a plantation store stocked with such goods as meat, flour, tobacco, calico, and shoes. Slaves were debited for purchases at the store and received credits for the sale of their corn and for such work as making hogsheads and chopping wood. In 1858 some of the Bringier Negroes had accumulated credits ranging as high as $50 to $100.[25] On James Hamilton Couper's Georgia plantation, twenty-one selected male slaves were allotted an entire field to till for their own benefit and given half of each Saturday to work their crop. Closely supervised the first year, they divided net proceeds amounting to some $1500. But left to their own devices thereafter, they soon lost interest in the experiment, and Couper, a truly exceptional master, was obliged to abandon his attempt to instill greater self-reliance in his slaves.[26]

Other incentives were pegged directly to work performance. A special present, usually an article of clothing, might be given as a reward to an individual slave who had picked the highest amount of cotton or who had consistently been first on watch during grinding season.[27] On occasion, the entire work force might receive special compensation for an unusually productive effort. Thus, when the Bringier sugar plantations yielded a bumper crop in 1852, the family's New Orleans factor suggested that silver coins be distributed among the hands by way of reward. "The Crop has been a large one," wrote Martin Gordon, Jr. "The boys have no doubt worked well, and a little money given to them, would do good."[28] Perhaps the motive for such gestures was purely economic, but, if Professor Genovese would allow us to postulate gratitude among those of unequal status, I would suggest that perhaps a particle of gratitude was reflected in this instance.

By modern standards, public health conditions in the nineteenth century were appallingly bad. Especially was this true in the antebellum South, where the hot climate combined with a rural society to exacerbate an already difficult situation. The mortality rate, particularly among infants, was frightfully high. Some measure of the problem may be gained from this terse entry by the overseer of Duncan Kenner's Ashland sugar plantation: "From Jany 1st 1845 to Jany 1st 1852 there has bin 86 Births *and 47 of them is now dead.*"[29] But disease and death afflicted whites as well as blacks. Anyone conversant with the traditional sources knows that the two ubiquitous topics in the correspondence of that era were health and the weather.

There is ample evidence in the records of antebellum planters to support the judgment of William D. Postell that the health care accorded slaves "was no better and no worse than that of the populace as a whole for that period."[30] Most slaveholders evinced genuine concern for the physical welfare of their Negroes. Minor ailments were usually treated by the master or overseer, but trained physicians were called in to diagnose and prescribe for more serious cases of slave illness. Expenditures for these professional services often contributed significantly to plantation overhead. Some proprietors contracted with medical practitioners to attend all cases on the plantation at a fixed annual rate. F. D. Richardson, a Bayou Têche sugar planter, entered into such an arrangement in 1848, agreeing to pay a neighboring doctor $150 to do the practice of his Bayside plantation for the year. Four years later, Maunsel White contracted to pay $250 for the like service on his Deer Range estate, stipulating that "the Doct. is to visit the plantation twice a Week positively Sick or no Sick & when any Sick as often as required." Another Louisiana planter, Colonel Joseph A. S. Acklen, apparently employed two physicians on a fulltime basis to minister to the needs of the 700 slaves on his six cotton plantations.[31]

It was a more common practice, however, to engage physicians only as they were needed to treat individual cases. Charges for a single visit ranged from $1 to as high as $25.[32] The annual cost of medical services performed on an individual case basis usually approximated the amount paid by those who contracted for such services at a specified rate. For example, Henry McCall, proprietor of an Ascension Parish sugar estate with a slave force of about 150, paid $310 to a single physician for the latter's attendance upon his Negroes during the year 1823. Similarly, Judge Thomas Butler spent $177 in a six-months period for medical services rendered to slaves on one of his plantations. The cost of treating a single slave sometimes reached astonishing dimensions. Thus, after paying eighteen visits to a young Negro whose arm had been mangled in a cotton gin, a Mississippi physician presented the owner with a bill for nearly $130.[33]

Certainly, a great deal of such solicitude for the physical welfare of southern slaves can be attributed to economics. After all, slaves were property, and the loss of a valuable hand hit the planter where it hurt—in the pocketbook. But I suggest that there is more to it than that, that many masters were genuinely concerned about their Negroes as human beings. Sir Charles Lyell perceived as much when, following a visit to James Hamilton Couper's Hopeton plantation, he noted that Mrs. Couper frequently was obliged to sit up all night with a sick Negro child. "In submitting to this," remarked the astute Lyell, "they are actuated by mixed motives—a feeling of kindness, and a fear of losing the services of a slave."[34] Those same "mixed motives" presumably influenced the

WILLIAM K. SCARBOROUGH   117

Virginia proprietor who sent his blacksmith to the Hot Springs for three weeks to relieve the latter's rheumatism; or the Louisiana planter who directed that a valued hand "be sent to the sea shore" to convalesce after a bout with the whooping cough.[35]

The deep emotional attachment and genuine Christian compassion with which many owners regarded their slaves are perhaps most clearly reflected in those passages which record the death of a beloved servant. Representative of a number of such notations in the papers of Maunsel White are the following:

[October 30, 1856] Poor Clem died on Tuesday evening after 2½ days of illness with an Inflamation of the Bowells. a good & truthful & faithful & Honest Boy. May eternal happiness be his portion in an Other World.

[December 17, 1858] last night about 11 o.k. Poor Ralph died after a long lingering Illness. a good & faithful servant. may the Almighty Power give his spirit rest for ever in Heaven.

[September 7, 1860] Buried Poor Celeste near her Father & mother. a youthful mother herself leaving two small children & regretted by several of her fellow servants & also her master & mistress may the Allmighty receive her Soul in Bliss.[36]

Dr. Martin W. Philips, proprietor of a model Mississippi cotton estate, manifested similar sentiments when he lamented the passing of a Negro boy in these words: "[September 23, 1855] Died this morning . . . Scott, Emily's next to oldest boy—a remarkable child of his age, a pet of us all. I feel as if I had lost some dear relative. We know he is the better by the change. May God make us all resigned and able to say, 'Thy will, O god, be done.' "[37] Not even supposedly callous overseers were immune from betraying such maudlin sentimentality upon the death of a favorite Negro. Thus, Louisiana overseer Moore Rawls, in a letter to his absentee employer, gave this moving account of the demise of one Isaac:

Isaac was a good Servant and I believe a good man. and one too
who I never had to inflict any punishment on. we done all we could
for him, but Oh the pale Horse would paw at his door, until the
Scyth of time Clip the brittle thread of life. now he is gone. Blessed
are dead that die in the Lord. it was a Solom Sight to See at least
140 Negroes, following his remains to the place of interment.
Fannie [Rawls' wife] could not help sheding tears.[38]

To deny, in the face of expressions like these, that southern whites
were capable of treating their slaves with genuine warmth and
compassion is to miss a vital part of the master–slave relationship
in the Old South.

Beyond doubt, the most reprehensible feature of domestic slavery was the separation of black families through sale and will. To
argue that many slaveholders exerted every effort to preserve the
integrity of their black families does not alter the fact that such
divisions occurred, and probably on a larger scale than that
suggested by the statistical manipulations of Fogel and Engerman.
Yet, even here, there were examples of compassionate understanding by sensitive masters. Thus, Maunsel White, who normally adhered to the inflexible policy of never selling a slave, was
moved to relent when approached by a fellow planter who sought
to purchase one of his female servants in order to reunite her with
her husband. White explained his philosophy in the following
letter:

As to selling you the negroes that you wish to purchase from me;
I would do it willingly if I had not made myself a solemn promise
never to sell a negroe   it is a trafic I have never done   I would
rather give them their liberty than sell them. . . . & yet I should
not like to deprive Hector of his wife if they love each other & are
worthy people & also provided she feels no desire to go with her
children   in such a case & to make those poor people happy, I
would let you have her at whatever she was considered to be worth
by any two disinterested persons.[39]

It is not clear from the context of the letter whether or not White
owned the children to whom he refers. If he did, I must, in

fairness, concede that his solicitude for the happiness of Hector and his spouse did not override economic interest to the extent that he was willing to part with their children.

In some cases, masters endeavored to mitigate the emotional anguish which often attended the separation of black families by serving as amanuenses for slaves who sought to communicate with distant relatives. One such slaveholder was Lewis Thompson of North Carolina, who carried on a regular correspondence in behalf of some of his slaves who had close relatives in Virginia. In response to a letter written for Lawrence, a young Negro boy, to his mother in King and Queen County, Virginia, Thompson received a heart-rending communication from the mother's owner. It began with an admonition from the mother for her son to obey his master:

> [S]he was very much distressed to hear that he had failed to do his work as he ought to have done, and for fear of being whiped had run off for a short time, she wishes you to say to him, that she hopes for her sake that he will never let it be the case again; that he will try and do all he can to please his master; she also wishes you to say to him that he must never take any thing that does not belong to him, from white or black; his mother sends her best love to him, and also all of his relatives, and hope he may please his master and get along well; she hopes you will write for him again as soon as you receive this letter; she sends him, enclosed, a small piece of money, ten cents, and if he will be a good boy and behave himself, she will try and send him more in her next letter; his mother requests me to write you his age, he was 12 years old the 30th of last September.[40]

This poignant letter has many interesting aspects. Some will see in it a calculated effort on the part of the two slaveholders to instill discipline in the boy by manipulating the words of his mother. To the contrary, I think the latter's admonition is genuine. In addition, the letter casts some doubt upon Genovese's contention that masters, either through indifference or deliberate intent, contrived to keep their slaves ignorant of their ages.[41] As this communication suggests, many owners simply did not know the ages of their servants, especially those acquired through purchase. Above all, this missive illustrates the deep emotional ties which existed within the black family and the tragedy of tearing asunder those families. Yet, at the same time, it tells us something about the character of the white masters who facilitated such correspondence.

Thus far, I have emphasized primarily the benevolent aspects of the slave regime. There was, of course, another side—that of discipline and punishment. No matter how kindly and compassionate they might be under ordinary circumstances, all planters insisted upon discipline, order, and strict adherence to plantation rules and regulations. The best evidence of superior slave management—as the James River planter, Hill Carter, once observed—was the maintenance of "good discipline with little or no punishment."[42] Unfortunately, this ideal was seldom realized. Rules were broken and the transgressors were punished. The slaveholders repeatedly enjoined their subordinates to be firm, impartial, and dispassionate in their chastisement of offending Negroes; or, as William J. Minor put it, to punish in a "gentlemanly manner."[43] But, like the slave codes themselves, such injunctions were violated more often than they were observed.

Whipping, although distasteful to some, was the most common mode of punishment. Most planters limited the number of lashes which could be applied at any one time to a refractory slave. The most common maximum was fifty, but more indulgent masters specified much lower limits. Thus, Georgia planter George Jones Kollock and Plowden Weston, proprietor of a large South Carolina rice estate, prohibited punishments which exceeded ten and fifteen lashes, respectively. In order to diminish the likelihood of whippings being administered in a sudden passion, Weston further advised his overseers that it was "desirable to allow 24 hours to elapse between the discovery of the offense, and the punishment."[44] Notwithstanding such safeguards, the sound of the whip and the cries of its victims reverberated across the

WILLIAM K. SCARBOROUGH   121

Southland where it was the standard instrument of punishment on virtually all plantations. And if many southern slaves escaped its direct effect, all suffered from the omnipresent fear which even its occasional use inspired.

In the final analysis, the quality of life enjoyed by southern blacks depended, in large measure, upon the character of their individual masters. If there were many indulgent and compassionate slaveowners—men like Couper of Georgia, Jenkins of Mississippi, Polk and White of Louisiana, Allston and Weston of South Carolina—who exemplified to the highest degree those traits best described by the appellation "southern gentleman," there were also hard-headed businessmen like George Washington, who has been characterized by none other than Ulrich B. Phillips as "one of the least tolerant employers and masters who put themselves upon record,"[45] and downright sadists, such as Bennet H. Barrow and the first Wade Hampton. The extremes may, perhaps, best be illustrated by contrasting the attitudes and practices of two Louisiana planters, Maunsel White and Bennet H. Barrow.

A native of Ireland, White came to New Orleans in 1801 and soon became a successful commission merchant.[46] Like so many other business and professional men in the Old South, he was influenced by the agrarian ideal and, as the years passed, he began to invest his surplus capital in land and slaves. By the mid-1840s, having acquired an interest in at least four sugar and cotton plantations in southern Louisiana, White retired from the active management of his factorage firm in order to devote all his energies to these planting enterprises. He established his residence at Deer Range, a large sugar estate in Plaquemines Parish with a slave force of more than 200. For some twenty years thereafter, ending with his death in 1863, White was one of the major sugar producers in south Louisiana.

Although he vigorously supported and defended the institution of slavery, White did all in his power to mitigate its evils. Even-tempered, just, compassionate, and devoutly religious, he was a true patriarch to the members of his black family. Reference has already been made to his concern for the physical well-being of his slaves, to his fixed policy of never selling a Negro, and to the deep sorrow which he manifested upon the death of faithful servants. Many other examples might be cited to illustrate White's genuine concern for the health and happiness of his black charges. On one occasion, he deviated from the standard practice in Louisiana during rolling season by stopping work the day after Christmas and giving "all the People . . . Several gallons of wine for their Comfort & the whole of the evening for recreation." Another time, when apprised by overseer James N. Bracewell of a serious outbreak of measles on Concord, his absentee cotton plantation, White instructed his subordinate to take good care of the Negroes, *"let what may happen to the crop."* Several months later, when Bracewell engaged a keel boat, at a cost of $350, to help transfer the Concord slaves and stock to a new plantation on Bayou Latanache, White expressed pleasure with the arrangement, observing that "the people will be protected from the weather & wont have to trudge in the mud & sleep out."[47] Relatively inconsequential in themselves, such expressions when taken together bespeak human compassion of an uncommonly high order in the one who articulated them.

Despite these manifestations of paternalistic benevolence, White, like others of his class, was also a strict disciplinarian when the occasion demanded. Although he once confided to his son, "I dont like to whip," the lash was employed on the White plantations to chastise those deemed guilty of such offenses as inefficient work, "willful lieing," and "feigning illness." However, runaways were few, and White probably came nearer than most to achieving the optimum condition of firm discipline with a minimum of punishment. Perhaps, in the case of Maunsel White and others like him, there was more than a particle of truth in the charge which he leveled against the South's enemies during the early days of the Civil War. "Behold," said he, "Northern English, & French

Fanatics make war upon us because we own slaves & treat them so much better than they do their Labouring Classes, who have the Freedom to starve."[48]

But if White typified the planter class at its best, his fellow Louisianian Bennet H. Barrow projected quite a different image. It is surprising—indeed, astonishing—that Fogel and Engerman should have chosen the latter to document their case for the benign treatment of southern slaves;[49] for Barrow, the proprietor of a large West Feliciana Parish cotton plantation, was one of the most sadistic masters of whom there is any record.[50] To be sure, he accorded his slaves many of the customary privileges. He gave generous allowances, long holidays—sometimes as much as two weeks at Christmas—and rewards to those who worked well. He also permitted occasional dinners and dances during the course of the year. But there were also many restrictions. Barrow refused to allow his Negroes to marry off the plantation; he severely restricted their freedom of movement; he denied them the right to attend preaching; and he refused to permit them to cultivate gardens or raise chickens, believing that such a privilege would undermine his exclusive claim upon their time.

Although he was fair to those who labored diligently and adhered to plantation regulations, Barrow was a firm believer in rigid discipline and dealt harshly with those who violated the rules. His philosophy of slave management is best exemplified by the following comment: "am sattisfied the best plan is to give them every thing they require for their comfort and never that they will do without Whipping or some punishment."[51] And punish he did; indeed, he seemed to view it almost as a sport. In both the variety and severity of punishment, Barrow seems almost unmatched among southern slaveowners. His plantation diary reveals that, among other iniquities, he frequently ordered general whippings, threatened to shoot runaways—and on at least one occasion carried out his threat—encouraged dogs to bite cornered runaways, confined slaves in chains, and sanctioned ducking as a form of punishment. The following entries depict instances of unusually brutal treatment on Barrow's Highland plantation:

[March 6, 1840] My driver sent for me this morning   Lize & Fanny had a fight last night—gave them three oake switches each—and made them Fight it out—they seemed quit sick of it—after one switch was gone.

[June 12, 1844] Demps has been doing nothing since last November   Dr. King tending him for Loss of his Eye sight, gave him up—to appearance seemed as well as ever   gave him 25 cuts yesterday morning & ordered him to work Blind or not. to show the scoundrel. has run off—will make him see sights as Long as I live.

[September 16, 1841] Ginney Jerry ran off Last Thursday to day week, after being shot, Will shoot to kill him should I be fortunate enoughf to meet him, Will sell him &c.[52]

It is possible that Barrow's bark was a bit worse than his bite, for the chronic troublemaker Ginney Jerry returned to plague his master on other occasions during the remaining years covered by the diary. Still, one cannot avoid the conclusion that Barrow's concept of paternalism was to treat his slaves more like animals than human beings. Fortunately, if the extant plantation records are representative of the whole, Barrow was not only an unworthy, but an atypical, member of the southern planter class.

Although I have here tried to view the institution of slavery from the perspective of the slaveholding class, I would be remiss if I did not consider briefly the role played by the slaves in defining the limits of the system. For, as Professors Blassingame and Genovese have so ably demonstrated, the latter exerted great influence in determining the guidelines under which they lived and labored. The master and his slaves were integral parts of the same community. Although the former, by law, exercised absolute power, the latter were constantly probing, continually challenging the limits of that authority—converting privileges into rights, helping to define policy, vetoing the selection of drivers and overseers. It was this arrangement that made life bearable for most plantation slaves; and knowing this, the planters readily acquiesced in the game.

However, for many masters, it was more than a game—more than just a device to promote harmony and order. A great many southern slaveholders earnestly solicited advice from their slaves and relied heavily upon both their individual and collective judgments as human beings. This is clearly discernible in the correspondence between plantation agents and their absentee employers. For example, in apprising Virginia planter John Hartwell Cocke of a request from a neighboring slave to marry a female servant on Cocke's Alabama plantation, the steward wrote: "Mr Borden's Boy (Washington) has a letter to me I learn, consenting for him to take a wife here. What say you? The servants don't wish it."[53] Although the final decision obviously rested with Cocke, there is a clear implication that slave opinion carried considerable weight. Similarly, a Mississippi agent reporting on the progress of a new overseer informed his North Carolina employer that "from what I have seen and can learn from the negroes . . . [I think] he will do well. They are all satisfied with him."[54] Once again, the judgment of the Negroes was solicited and reported to their master.

But the slaves did much more than merely offer their counsel on matters of policy. They made their greatest inroads upon the authoritarian character of the white power structure by deliberately exploiting natural antipathies among personnel in the managerial hierarchy—e.g., between driver and overseer, overseer and master. Perhaps the most serious deficiency in my own monograph on the overseer was my failure to give proper emphasis to the role of the Negroes in sowing discord between proprietor and manager. Yet, there are countless examples of plantation slaves promoting such disharmony in order to ameliorate the psychological and material conditions of their daily lives.

Whenever a new overseer was employed, there was invariably a period of testing as the slaves sought to determine how much they could get away with under the new regime. Such an incident was reported by Louisiana planter Thomas Butler during a brief visit to his Grand Caillou sugar plantation.

> . . . some of the negroes are endeavouring to try the mettle & temper of the new overseer. Ned gave him some trouble & threatened not to live under his management. He is usually a quiet well disposed negro & may possibly have been put forward by some of the others. . . . I have told them all that the overseer would require nothing unreasonable from them & that they must submit to his authority. I am much pleased with his management but fear that he will have some difficulty when I leave . . . . I will however get Pierce [Butler's son] to ride down occasionally until Mr. Courquill is fairly established in authority.[55]

If, after the initial period of testing, the Negroes were satisfied with their new manager, affairs usually proceeded smoothly and there were few disciplinary problems. In the contrary event, the disgruntled slaves might seek to oust the overseer by acts of massive disobedience or, if circumstances did not warrant such extreme action, to undermine his authority and mitigate the harshness of his regime by carrying complaints directly to the owner.

Typical of the tactics employed by southern slaves to promote suspicion and mutual distrust between master and overseer was an incident which occurred on an absentee South Carolina plantation owned by John Berkley Grimball. At the behest of the driver, a Negro messenger, whose function it was to carry communications between owner and manager at biweekly intervals, reported to Grimball that the overseer had exhausted his stock of provisions, had put up the cotton in a damp state, and was feeding his brother's horse out of the proprietor's cornhouse. Terming the latter "an absolute *Outrage*," the owner fired off an angry letter to his overseer, William McKendree. Less than a week later, the driver suddenly appeared with the story that McKendree, infuriated by receipt of the above letter, had accused him of sending detrimental reports about his management to Grimball and had broken him as driver. Grimball, now thoroughly aroused, ordered the driver reinstated, asserting that "the right of Making and displacing drivers is one which no one has a liberty to exercise without my permission." With his job clearly in jeopardy, McKendree hastened to Charleston where he was able to convince Grimball that the charges lodged against him were untrue. "I certainly felt relieved," remarked the proprietor, "and very rejoiced to find that McKendree was entitled to the confidence which for four years I had reposed in him."[56] In this instance the Negroes failed in their ploy, but, more often than not, their efforts were crowned with success.

Most planters were well aware of the divisive techniques utilized by their ingenious black wards. Observing that "the master and overseer should always pull at the same end of the rope," Hill Carter warned that "Negroes soon discover any little jarring" between the two, "and are sure to take advantage of it."[57] Nevertheless, much to the consternation of plantation managers all over the South, most slaveholders permitted—and some explicitly directed—their Negroes to carry complaints over the head of the overseer to the master.[58] To comprehend why they did so, it is only necessary to understand the relative positions occupied by owner and manager under the slave system. As William Postell has pointed out, the overseer was "the symbol of the hardest features of slavery." It was he "who had to absorb the bitterness of bondage" as felt by those whose labors he directed.[59] The planter, on the other hand, precisely because of the presence of a hired intermediary who could "take the heat," was enabled to assume the role of benevolent protector to the members of his black family. Thus, just as the policeman of today is often reviled as "pig" and the judge revered as an impartial arbiter, so too was the overseer an object of contempt and hatred while his employer commanded respect and often genuine affection.

In essence, then, the practice of affording southern slaves a direct avenue of appeal to their masters, or the latter's agents, acted as a safety valve, imparting flexibility to the system and alleviating frustrations which were potentially explosive. The point is well illustrated by a communication from an Alabama steward to his absentee employer in Virginia. Discussing the installation of a new overseer, he wrote: "Mr Carter speaks kindly & acts kindly toward them & I see they begin to feel it, but *it is important* for them *to Know I am ready* to *see them if necessary.*" For their part, the overseers could only protest and accept with resignation a situation over which they had little control. Thus, the veteran manager of Colonel John S. Preston's giant Houmas sugar estate recorded an infraction of plantation discipline in these terse words: "Jacob Ran off for nothing   thinking Col Preston will be hear Soon and he will not be punished." [60] In my judgment, the safety-valve concept explains, at least in part, why the vast majority of large slaveholders elected to retain the overseer system despite all its deficiencies and why insensitive planters, like Bennet Barrow, who dispensed with the services of white overseers had so many disciplinary problems.

Because of the sense of justice, honor, and noblesse oblige which induced many planters to treat their slaves with humanity and compassion, and because the system was flexible enough to allow the slaves a role in defining its limits, most southern Negroes were able to accommodate to the institution of chattel slavery. Those who could not, of course, were obliged to explore other alternatives. Perhaps the most common form of resistance was that of simply taking flight. One must be careful not to read too much into this act of disobedience which was endemic on southern plantations. A great many runaways may be attributed to the natural fear of punishment for some dereliction in work, much as a child who accidentally breaks a favorite lamp may run away and hide in order to delay the inevitable consequence of his act. But on many plantations there were a few Negroes who absconded repeatedly, thereby earning the reputation of being chronic malcontents. Such conduct was indicative of an incapacity on their part to adapt to the system. Infrequently, general dissatisfaction within a particular slave force was manifested in mass runaways, which usually had the desired effect of producing some change in management on the affected unit. Except in the latter case, most slaveholders—at least in the Deep South where the possibility of permanent escape was remote—accepted these periodic acts of defiance and discontent with relative equanimity. To be sure, they expressed annoyance and soundly thrashed the offenders upon their return, but the runaways caused them little mental anguish; such acts were simply one of the hazards of their business.

On occasion, southern blacks resorted to more serious acts of resistance. Scattered throughout the antebellum records are numerous reports of inexplicable fires, which leveled ginhouses, barns, and other outbuildings, often resulting in losses to the owners amounting to many thousands of dollars. Doubtless, some of these conflagrations resulted from accidental causes, but many were deliberate acts of arson perpetrated by disaffected slaves. The problem became so serious in one Louisiana neighborhood that night watches were instituted on some plantations to guard against such incendiary acts.[61] Ironically, most masters, confident of the loyalty and docility of their Negroes, were loath to believe them capable of committing such heinous crimes. Thus, when a series of mysterious fires erupted on Edmund Ruffin's Marlbourne estate in the late 1850s, after he had relinquished control of the place to his son-in-law William Sayre, the former master was utterly at a loss to explain the motivation or identity of the incendiaries. When neighbors suggested that Marlbourne Negroes might be the culprits, Ruffin responded heatedly that he did "not believe a tittle of such deductions from premises which I know to be entirely false." But, several years later, he learned the truth. It seems that the Marlbourne slaves could not adjust to the new proprietary arrangement under which five Ruffin children acted as co-partners of the estate with Sayre as the resident manager. Consequently, "prompted by dislike of their new & singular con-

dition as to ownership, & to dislike to be governed by Mr. Sayre,"
they resorted to arson in the hope that "such great destruction of
property by fire would induce a breaking up of the existing arrangement, & the division of the slaves among owners in sever-
alty."[62] Characteristically, Ruffin attached little blame to his
slaves for their incendiary activities; rather, he held himself responsible for creating the circumstances which prompted them to
act out of a sense of frustration and desperation.

The ultimate act of slave resistance, of course, was open insurrection. For reasons which Professor Genovese has brilliantly
delineated,[63] there were few such outbreaks in the Old South. But
if few actually materialized, the threat was always present, and the
memory of St. Domingo loomed large in the minds of most southern whites.[64] Outwardly, however, they professed absolute
confidence in their security and ridiculed northerners for suggesting that the slaves were dissatisfied and potentially rebellious.
They reported with evident relish that they normally slept behind
unlocked doors and windows. Yet, it is impossible to reconcile this
façade of outward calm with the paroxysm of fear and outrage
which swept over the South in the wake of such actual uprisings as
the Nat Turner affair and John Brown's raid on Harpers Ferry.

In the days immediately following the Turner insurrection,
according to Edmund Ruffin, "terror & fear so affected most
persons as to produce a condition of extended & very general
community-insanity."[65] Wild rumors were circulated. Thousands
of slaves, from central Virginia to southern North Carolina, were
said to be implicated, and some even intimated that the conspiracy
extended into the Southwest. In distant Natchez, Stephen Duncan confided to his brother-in-law, Judge Thomas Butler: "I do not
credit the story of the extension of the Virginia insurrection tho' I
have great apprehension that we will one day have our threats out
in this country. We have here 5 blacks to one white; and within 4
hours march of Natchez there are 2200 able bodied male slaves. It
behooves [us] to be vigilant—but *silent*."[66] The injunction to si-

lence was heeded in the case of actual uprisings—e.g., there was no mention of the Turner affair in the Charleston newspapers— but reports of alleged plots and conspiracies appeared frequently in the press and served to keep southern whites in a state of almost perpetual uneasiness. Thus, following the detection of an alleged conspiracy in East Feliciana Parish, Louisiana, on Christmas Eve, 1835, a New Orleans correspondent wrote: "Great excitement prevails through the country. The citizens of St. Francisville and West and East Feliciana, are all in arms, and patrolling the country, and the planters, many of them coming into town for safety."[67] In light of such evidence, there can be no doubt that the fear of slave uprisings had a profound psychological impact upon whites living in the antebellum South.

Ultimately, the burden of slavery proved too heavy a cross for the white South to bear. In the end, it was not the slaves, but their masters, who rose in rebellion. In their frantic zeal to preserve their "peculiar institution" in the face of increasingly hostile world opinion and, more particularly, against the wishes of a majority of their own countrymen, the slaveholders risked all on the desperate gamble of secession. Many southern whites are still reluctant to admit that the War for Southern Independence was fought in behalf of slavery. To attribute the war to such a cause is somehow to tarnish the image of the glorious Confederacy. So, when such an interpretation is advanced, they bristle with righteous indignation and talk of states' rights, the tariff, insuperable economic differences, and the like. Nevertheless, it is evident from the contemporary literature—public speeches, private correspondence, diaries, newspaper editorials, even proceedings of the secession conventions—that slavery was the overriding issue in the minds of most articulate southerners. The abolitionist crusade, attempts to restrict the spread of slavery, repeated violations of the federal fugitive slave law, John Brown's raid, election of the "black Republican" Lincoln—those were the events which inflamed the South and drove her out of the Union.

Certainly, the slaveholders understood what the real issue was. Never was it stated more clearly than by Edmund Ruffin when, on the day of the 1860 presidential election, he wrote:

This is the day for the election of electors—the momentous election which, if showing the subsequent election of Lincoln to be certain, will serve to show whether these southern states are to remain free, or to be politically enslaved—whether the institution of negro slavery, on which the social & political existence of the south rests, is to be secured by our resistance, or to be abolished in a short time, as the certain result of our present submission to northern domination.[68]

A month and a half later, John Berkley Grimball of South Carolina indicated that he too was cognizant of the fundamental issue which had brought his state to the brink of secession. "The Prospect before us in regard to our Slave property, if we continue in the Union," he said, "is nothing less than utter ruin—The people have therefore with unexampled unanimity resolved to secede and to dare any consequence that may follow the act."[69] Thus did the slaveholders cast the die which, within the space of four short years, would leave their world in a shambles.

For many southerners, the moment of truth concerning the true feelings of their black wards came during the ensuing Civil War. They were appalled when supposedly loyal and trustworthy blacks began to flee in droves to the approaching Yankees, and they lashed out at what they regarded as the ingratitude of their slaves. There had been occasional grumblings of a similar character even before the war. An example may be cited from the correspondence of Stephen Duncan. When asked by the owner to investigate reports of slave discontent on a neighboring absentee plantation, Duncan could find no discernible cause for the unrest which had culminated in a recent attempt on the overseer's life. "There is no gratitude among them," exploded Duncan. "I know not why these people sh[oul]d be dissatisfied with Wilson [the overseer]. He is certainly a humane man, and as kind & attentive to them when sick, as to his own child. He is not too severe—on the contrary he is reasonable & mild."[70]

But it was the mass desertions of the Civil War which finally brought home to southern whites the painful truth that those smiling black faces did not necessarily reflect deep-seated contentment with the system. For many, it was a shattering realization. As Virginia slaves began absconding en masse to the enemy during General George McClellan's peninsular campaign in the spring of 1862, a stunned Edmund Ruffin could only express astonishment at "the delusion of the negroes." Several months later, as the Yankee tide receded from the peninsula, most of the runaways began to return. But the master–slave relationship would never again be quite the same. On returning to his Pamunkey River plantation near Richmond, Ruffin confided these thoughts to his diary:

I approached & reached Marlbourne with painful feelings. . . . Since [last here] . . . great misfortunes have occurred. The general rebellion of the slaves . . . was without exception other than two of the house servants belonging to Mr. Sayre. . . . it is to me very painful to meet my former slaves, to whom I was attached by ties of affection on their part (as I believed) as well as on mine, under such changed circumstances. It will also be difficult for me to preserve towards them the same manner as if they had not offended.[71]

Despite these misgivings, the Marlbourne owners granted a general amnesty to their Negroes, and, at least on the surface, relations continued as before until the next Union incursion.

Other slaveholders were less charitable. The deep resentment and bitterness engendered among members of the slaveholding class by the wartime conduct of southern blacks are reflected in the following excerpt from the plantation book of Louis Manigault, one of the great South Carolina rice planters:

This war has taught us the perfect impossibility of placing the least Confidence in any Negro. In too numerous instances those we esteemed the most have been the first to desert us. . . . For my own part I am more than ever Convinced that the only suitable occupation for the Negro is to be a laborer of the Earth, and to work as a field Hand upon a well disciplined plantation. It has now been proven also that those planters who were the most indulgent to their Negroes when we were at peace, have Since the Commencement of the war encountered the greatest trouble in the management of this Species of property.[72]

Perhaps, as Genovese has suggested, gratitude is possible only among equals, or perhaps the longing for freedom and human dignity which welled in the bosoms of southern slaves simply outweighed their gratitude for past benevolences. Whatever the explanation, the experiences in the Civil War revealed, more clearly than any others until the recent civil rights revolution, the basic dichotomy of thought that still prevails in the South between blacks and whites.

As the war progressed and the northern armies pressed slowly, but inexorably, into the southern heartland, a pall of gloom descended over the region. Gone was the heady exuberance of those early months when there was universal confidence in the ultimate success of the Confederacy. By the latter part of 1862, with much of the West in Union hands and the recent offensive thrusts of Lee and Bragg blunted by superior northern armies, it had become apparent to many that the days of the slaveholders' regime were numbered. Two brief entries in the diary of Alexander Pugh, a wealthy sugar planter and ardent secessionist, reflect the growing despair of that dying civilization. On November 20, he wrote: "Times are very gloomy, and the future promises to be worse." A week later, he was even more despondent. "I stay at home all the time," he remarked, "having very little or nothing to do—but to think over the past, and speculate on the future."[73]

But it remained for the venerable Edmund Ruffin to deliver what Clement Eaton has called an "elegy on the passing of the Old South."[74] As McClellan's huge army neared the opposite bank of the James River, Ruffin paused to take one last look at his deserted homestead. These were his words and thoughts on that moving occasion:

After breakfast I rode . . . to see Beechwood in its present deserted & desolate condition. I chose to be alone. I went into every apartment of the mansion, as well as into my own in the old house. . . . In the mansion, all the furniture as yet remains. But the removal of the curtains, pictures, & other ornaments, gives an appearance of desolation greater than would an entirely emptied house. Every apartment brought to my mind some tender recollections, & especially the death chamber of my daughter Jane. About the mansion, & elsewhere on all the farm, I saw no human being, except an old negro woman in the dairy, churning . . . & a negro child sitting in the door of one of the few houses now occupied by the remaining old or infirm slaves. Afterwards I walked or rode through the lovely grounds near & below the house—the garden, the thinned & open woods, & the Wilderness. It was a melancholy gratification. I do not expect to see them again while existing circumstances continue, & the residents are exiles from their dearly loved & beautiful home. Next I went to the site of my old residence on Coggin's Point, now undistinguished from the remainder of the rich wheat-field of which it forms a part, except by the shade trees which ornamented the former yard, & most of which I planted. The wheat is already so much fallen, that even if there was labor for the harvest, half the value would be lost. There will be no such attempt . . . . The few negroes left merely attend to the remaining live-stock, until all can be moved away. I next visited the burial ground, & read over the inscriptions of the head-stones, concisely & simply stating the names, & dates of birth & death, of the dear ones whose remains were beneath. And here I addressed to God my customary daily prayers, & added others for the welfare of my family & country, & the restoration of that prosperity & happiness recently enjoyed . . . by both, and which have been so much reduced by the conduct of our vile public enemies.[75]

Thus did slavery die, and with it the civilization which had rested upon it. Forgotten are the virtues of that society and of the remarkable class which was its product. Only the legacy of bitterness, distrust, and racism remains to haunt us even unto this day.

Status and Social Structure in the Slave Community:

Evidence From New Sources

JOHN W. BLASSINGAME

The great scholar J. Winston Coleman in his 1940 study, *Slavery Times in Kentucky*, described many of the elements of status in the quarters accepted by historians. According to Coleman, the house servant was "one of the most desirable positions on the whole plantation. The house servants formed a class quite distinct from, and socially above, the field hands; in fact . . . they assumed an air of superiority over the field hands and sometimes refused to recognize them. . . . Also, slaves often rated their social standing by their value in the market." A number of historians added the mulatto, the driver, and the artisan to those accorded high status in the quarters. While Coleman typifies the traditional view, Kenneth Stampp has been the historian most sensitive to the true nature of slave social structure. Yet, he too contended in *The Peculiar Institution* that "domestics, artisans, and foremen constituted the aristocracy of slave society." In *The Slave Community* I agreed with the theory when I wrote: "those slaves who held some important post in the plantation hierarchy were ascribed higher status in the quarters than the mass of slaves."

This view of slave social structure is much too simplistic. The house servant, driver, mulatto, and artisan have been mistakenly placed at the top of the slave hierarchy because historians unwittingly assumed that a bondsman's status depended on two things—how much personal contact he had with the planter and how valuable his services were to the master. Since it enhanced the planter's ego to view a slave's status in this way, the plantation records usually relied upon by scholars are misleading when considering slave social structure.

Two steps must be taken in order for scholars to develop new ways of looking at slave social structure. First, of course, is more systematic exploration of sociological theory. Second, new sources on slave life must be examined. In preparing this study, I initially reviewed the black folklore collected by J. Mason Brewer, A. M. Christensen, Alan Dundes, and Elsie Clews Parsons. Then I turned to the Works Progress Administration era interviews recently compiled by George Rawick. I have, however, restricted my purview to that of the most reliable volume in the collection, Fisk University's *Unwritten History of Slavery*. Finally, I have used material from my own collection of slave letters, speeches, interviews, and autobiographies written between 1736 and 1938. What do these sources reveal about the accuracy of our traditional view of the roots of status in the slave community? How true, for example, is the proposition that light skin color played a significant role in status groupings in the quarters?

The slaves interviewed by Fisk University in 1929 refer so frequently to mulattoes as "yellow bitches" and the sons thereof that it is difficult to accept the proposition that simply being nearly white was any guarantee of status. On the contrary, it was a mark of degradation. Indeed, mulatto slaves expressed such hatred for their white fathers that light skin color was clearly as much of a liability as an advantage in the quarters. An Alabama bondswoman recalled that, although mulatto slaves thought they were better than blacks, she felt the "Lamp Black" slave was "de mos' 'pendable cau'se he is 'honest got.' " Others have made similar arguments. In an 1842 speech the Kentucky bondsman Lewis Clarke asserted, "The slaves used to debate together sometimes, what could be the reason the yellow folks couldn't be trusted like the dark ones could. As a general rule, they seemed to be dissipated, devil-may-care fellows; and I'll tell you what we concluded was the reason—we concluded it was because they was sons of their masters, and took after their fathers. . . . I have heard 'em talk on about it, . . . till I felt ashamed of the white blood that was in me."

Since practically all slaves distrusted house servants, it is illogical to assume that at the same time they accorded them great status. The degree of personal contact a slave had with whites was inversely related to his or her status in the quarters. A Tennessee house servant interviewed in 1929 observed that the other slaves "wouldn't say anything before me, 'cause I stayed in the house, and et in there, and slept in there." While it may have been attractive because of better and more food and clothing, the position of house servant was rejected by all blacks who had not been trained for it since childhood. The house servant was taught by the planter that he was superior to other blacks. The house servants included in the *Unwritten History of Slavery* constantly reiterated this point. "Mistress," one of them noted, "used to tell me not to play with the colored children so much 'cause I wasn't like they was." If the slave had grown up in the master's household, he often accepted such views. But many others saw that, inasmuch as they were socially confined and constantly under the surveillance of whites, they had the least desirable job on the plantation.

In addition to being forced to look upon a sea of white faces, the house servant, when compared to the field slave, led a sterile life. A former Mississippi slave declared: "I liked the field work better than I did the house work. We could talk and do anything we wanted to, just so we picked cotton; we used to sing and have lots of fun." Kenneth Stampp expressed the same idea in a different way when he noted that for the slave, "Living intimately with even a paternal master was not in all respects as completely satisfying as the whites liked to think." If historians move beyond the literal acceptance of the self-serving testimony of house servants and their masters, they may find the position of house servant at the very bottom of the slave's social ladder. House servants who achieved high standing among blacks did so in spite of their positions. Many of them had so many relatives and friends among the field hands that they could never identify totally with the master's interest. Consequently, when house servants were able to walk that thin line between maintaining the *appearance* of loyalty to masters with the *reality* of serving their fellow blacks, they ranked high as *individuals* in the black hierarchy.

From a psychological vantage point, as Eugene Genovese has pointed out, the driver was in an ambivalent position. That the slaves clearly understood this is revealed in the old Jamaican proverb "The driver flogs his own wife first." Still, the driver was usually too close to the master. Like the overseer, it was a hated position. Socially the driver was near the bottom of the slave hierarchy. An individual driver could move out of the depths only if he were skillful enough to protect the slaves.

The contentions of J. Winston Coleman notwithstanding, the price paid for a slave had little impact on his status. It is significant, for example, that rarely did any of the slaves in the Fisk compilation mention their sale price. Since being sold was such a painful and humiliating experience for slaves, few of them could take *any* pride in *any* aspect of the transaction. A Mississippi slave remembered her sale at age eleven with loathing: "They 'xamine you just like they do a horse; they look at your teeth, and pull your eyelids back and look at your eyes, and you feel just like you was a horse." She did not mention how much her new master paid for her. The blacks included in my research reacted the same way. The Reverend John Sella Martin wrote that on the occasion of his first sale it was difficult "to describe my despair or to make known my sense of humiliation at being put upon the auction block." The second time, when he was sold for $1700, Martin observed that he "ascended the auction-block—shall I say with shame? Yes; but this second time that I adorned this hideous medium of exchange I fear there was some hate mingled with my humiliation." In 1853, former Kentucky slave Lewis Hayden described the time when his master "sold all my brothers and sisters at auction. I stood by and saw them sold. When I was just going upon the block, he swapped me off for a pair of carriage-horses. I looked at those horses with strange feelings. . . . How I looked at those horses, and walked around them, and thought for *them* I was sold."

Many slaves thought it best not to talk about their sale price, because masters often equated how much labor blacks should perform with how much they had paid for them. Reflecting on this propensity of the plantation owners, a slave said that at her sale: "When my marster bought me he paid a heap o' money for me, eighteen hundred dollars. 'If you don' make dat money good what I pay for yer,' he said, 'you know what I do ter yer.' "

If the traditional view is incorrect, then what were the actual bases for status in the quarters? Although Professor Stampp discussed many of them in 1956, no historian has yet utilized his observations in any systematic attempt to analyze black social structure. Stampp stressed the loyalty of slaves to each other, their own internal class structure, and wrote that whatever masters did, "the stratification of slave society also resulted from an impelling force within the slaves themselves . . . the white caste's whole way of life was normally far beyond the reach of slaves. In slave society, therefore, success, respectability, and morality were measured by other standards, and prestige was won in other ways." While I reject Stampp's contention that the slaves' search for prestige was "pathetic," or that "the unlettered slaves rarely won distinction or found pleasure in intellectual or esthetic pursuits," his emphasis on the internal bases for status is correct. Analyses of social structure will never advance until this fact is accepted and a distinction is made between the roots of a slave's self-esteem and the basis of his status. There is, for instance, little light shed on social structure by Stampp's assertion that slave artisans and domestic servants obtained "a pleasant feeling of self-importance" from jobs well done.

However much personal gratification a bondsman obtained from a job, occupations translated into high social standing in the slave community only if they combined some of the following features: (1) mobility, which allowed the slave to leave the plantation frequently, (2) freedom from constant supervision by whites, (3) opportunity to earn money and (4) provision of a direct service to other blacks. Blacks who worked as drovers, teamsters, riverboatmen, carpenters, jockeys, blacksmiths, millwrights, shoemakers, seamstresses, distillers, and any slave who hired his own time gained status among other blacks because their jobs had one or more of these features. Occupation alone earned no one the top rung on the slave social ladder.

Despite all that historians have written in the past, slaves reserved the top rungs of the social ladder for those blacks who performed services for other slaves rather than for whites. However, slave social structure was so complex and so fluid, and the sources so misleading, that it is difficult to determine exactly who the social leaders were. Consider, for instance, the black preacher. Many historians have unthinkingly assigned the minister the highest social standing because religion seemed so crucial in all of the slave sources that have survived. The place of religion in slave life has been distorted, because most of the slave witnesses who recorded their stories of bondage were relatively old. Since the church has always been the refuge of the old, they may have overemphasized the importance of religion in their lives. With this *caveat* in mind, it is possible to examine dispassionately the relationship between service and status in the slave community.

At the top of the slave social ladder the conjuror and the preacher struggled for primacy. More often than not, the conjuror won. Claiming to have received his power from God, but believed by many to be in league with the devil, the conjuror was respected, feared, and appealed to by saints and sinners alike. Although many of the church-going blacks who talked to the white WPA interviewers in the 1930s disclaimed any belief in conjurors, they consistently said the opposite in the latter half of the nineteenth century. The former slaves interviewed between 1872 and 1900 reported an almost universal faith in the conjuror; he played a prominent role in black folk tales and received more deference than any other figure in the antebellum South. Generally, slaves bowed when they met him. A former slave reminiscing about the antebellum conjuror in the 1890s asserted that the slaves "worshipped him as if he were a priest."

Since the primary concern of all people in the nineteenth century was the maintenance of good health, the black physicians were near the top of the slave social structure. Midwives and those blacks with the greatest knowledge of the medicinal value of herbs and roots performed an important service in the quarters. One indication of their status was the constant complaint of southern whites that slaves consistently preferred to follow the advice of black root doctors rather than white physicians. The bondsman's concern over his health was, of course, one of the bases for the high social standing of the conjuror.

One of the most important ways for a slave to gain status was to be skilled in what folklorists call the verbal arts. The best practitioners of the verbal arts, according to one slave, were recognized as entertainers. He recalled in 1899 that a typical plantation party "would start off with a general greeting and conversation. Telling tales . . . was a common mode of entertaining. Next would come the guessing of riddles propounded by the more erudite portion of the company." Unfortunately, the party tales and riddles contained such explicit references to sex that the collectors either never heard or refused to print the more salacious ones.

Regardless of the stress laid on religion by old former slaves, the thoughts and actions of young plantation blacks, like most other youths, centered on sex, courtship, and marriage. To achieve any success in these areas, the slave had to be skilled in the verbal arts. Fortunately for the historian, nineteenth-century folklorists were keenly interested in slave courtship patterns. Courtship on the plantation was a battle of wits played by resort to riddles, poetic

144 Status and Social Structure in the Slave Community

boasting, toasts, and ridicule. Older slaves taught the young the complicated formulas. As Frank Banks recalled,

Among the slaves there were regular forms of "courtship," and almost every large plantation had an experienced old slave who instructed young gallants in the way in which they should go in the delicate matter of winning the girls of their choice. . . . "Uncle Gilbert" [the teacher on his plantation] held the very generally accepted opinion that "courtin' is a mighty ticklish bizness" and that he who would "git a gal wuth havin, mus' know how to talk fur her."

A few examples may illustrate the courtship formula. First, of course, a man had to find out if a woman was eligible by asking, "Kin' lady, since I have been trav'lin' up hill, vally an mountain, I nebber seed a lady dat suit my fancy mo' so den you does. Now is you a towel dat had been spun, or a towel dat had been woven? (Answer — if spun, single.)" Or he might say, "Are you a rag on the bush or a rag off the bush? (Answer — If a rag on the bush, free, if off, engaged.)"

Secondly, the slave seeking a partner had to ascertain whether he was an acceptable suitor. He would ask, "My dear kin' miss, has you any objections to me drawing my cher to yer side, and revolvin' de wheel of my conversation around de axle of your understandin'?" To demonstrate her acceptance of a suitor, the slave girl had to make a clever response to such questions. She might respond by saying: "I hears dat you is a dove flyin' from lim' to lim' wid no where to res' your weary wings. I's in de same condition an' hopes you kin fin' a place to res' you' heart." When accepted as a suitor, the slave then proceeded by a series of toasts and poetic allusions to convert the one of his choice:

Dear me, kin' Miss, you is de damsel of my eye,
Where my whole joy and pleasure lie.
If I has some money I'll give you a part,
If I has no money I'll give you my heart.

Once a successful courtship ended, there was a distinction made between couples on the basis of the way they were united. A "proper wedding," with a black or white minister officiating, was held in high esteem. A Missouri slave, Jennie Hill, said, "In the south . . . when a couple marries they just start living together without any ceremony. . . . But I was really married, My husband and I went to a slave on his place who could read and write and knew something of the Bible. . . . I was proud of my marriage . . . and I sure got mad when anybody said anything about us not being married."

Older slaves often demonstrated their verbal skills at church. Historians, folklorists, and novelists have often described the linguistic skills of the antebellum preacher. Few of them, however, have looked at the other members of the congregation. One of the primary marks of a slave's piety was his or her ability to bear public witness to God in the form of prayer. The person most adept at this, at making the congregation feel good, was always called upon to lead in prayer. In 1897, a former slave asserted, with some exaggeration, that during the antebellum period, "All that was required to make one good was to be able to pray a good prayer or to be a good singer." Religious testimony was so important that slaves reduced prayers to formulas and taught them to young converts. Intoned in a rhythmical melodious chant, these prayers employed fervid imagery and an impressive succession of metaphors and vivid pictures with pauses for audience response. A former slave remembered that at the night meetings on his plantation, a bondsman would offer the following prayer:

O! Lord here it is again and again and one time more that we thine weak an' unprofitable servants has permitted to bow, and I ask you while I make this feeble attempt to bow that you would bow my head below my knees, and my knees away down in some lonesome valley of humility where you have promised to hear and answer prayer at every time of need and every stressful hour for Jesus sake. (*Moan*)

We believe that love is growing old and sin is growing bold and Zion wheel is clogged and can't roll, neither can she put on her beautiful garments, but we ask you to come this way, seal her with love, type her with blood and send her around the hill sides clucking to her broods and bringing live sons and daughters to the marvelous light of thy glorious gospel as the bees to the honey comb and the little doves to the windows of Noah's ark, I pray thee. (*Moan*) . . . when I come down to death please rise our blood-bought spirits high and happy and our bodies be lowed to our mother dust for Christ sake. A-men. (*Long moans*)

The elite slaves in the quarters were the best singers and the creators of black music. Songs were such a crucial accompaniment of plantation labor, rowing boats, and husking corn, that a good singer might receive extra perquisites from his master. A writer in 1895 contended that "the singing of the slaves at work was regarded by their masters as almost indispensable to the quick and proper, performance of the labor, . . . that the leaders of the singing were often excused from work that they might better attend to their part of the business." Whether they sang spirituals, work songs, or dance songs, the singers joined those blacks most adept at playing musical instruments among the most respected entertainers in the quarters. Singers and musicians performed an important service in the slave community by providing solace to those wearied in mind and body.

Another group of creators also achieved status. They were the slaves who left their mark on the material culture—the slave woman who became a skilled seamstress and made beautiful quilts; the old man who could carve exquisite walking canes or whistles for youngsters; the bondsmen who made beautiful chairs, tables, beds, brooms, straw hats, and baskets; the woman who knew just the plants to use in dying cloth to make colorful clothes; the man who could make the best traps and seines; the women or men who were noted for their ability to prepare the most succulent rabbit, oppossum, raccoon, fish, barbecue, ginger cake, or molasses candy; and the person making the most potent wine, persimmon beer, cider, or whiskey. All stood high on the slave social ladder.

Nativity was one of the keys to status in the quarters. Every slave thought that work was lighter, masters kinder, and life better for blacks in his state than in any other. The former Louisiana bondsman, Alexander Kenner, testified in 1863, "The negroes in Mississippi are more stupid than those in Louisiana, on account of the masters being more cruel and oppressive." A Maryland slave's view was even more localized. Reporting that he had been to Virginia a few times, in 1863 he observed, "Slavery is harder down there than in Maryland. They have larger plantations and more servants, and they seem to be more severe. Down in Prince George's County, Md., they are a littler harder than they are in the upper part of the State." Slaves in the state, county or on the plantation generally ranked above those born outside these confines. The exception to the rule was native-born Africans who were revered by practically all blacks.

Cunning was another highly valued trait in the quarters. The bondsman who was a good hustler, cool cat, and confidence man in his effort to steal food for himself and others or who taught slaves how to avoid labor while appearing to work hard was held in high esteem in the slave community. In avoiding the lash, for example, youngsters learned from the cool cats that the way to make their quota of cotton was to pick as much as possible when the dew was still on it, to urinate on it, or to add rocks or watermelons to your pile and remove them before the cotton was ginned. The cool cat was the most frequent character in the slave folk tales. A consummate liar, a master at deceit, the cool cat was admired primarily because he was able to fool whites. Many of the jokes slaves told about themselves centered on the cool cat. He appears, for instance, in the story of the "Hog Thief":

Once an old slave used to make it his practice to steal hogs. The way he would be sure of the animal was he would tie one end of a rope around his prey and the other around himself. The old Negro had been successful for many years in his occupation, but one time when he caught one of his master's hogs he met his equal in strength. He was fixing to have a big time on the next day, which was Sunday. He was thinking about it and had the old hog going along nicely, but at last as he was coming up on the top of a very high hill the hog got unmanageable and broke loose from the old fellow's arms. Still the old man made sure it was all right because of the rope which tied them together, so he puffed and pulled and scuffed, till the hog got the best of him and started him to going down the steep hill. The hog carried him clear to his master's house, and the master and his family were sitting on the porch. All the Negro could say, as the hog carried him around and around the house by his master, was "Master, I come to bring your pig home!"

Teachers were highly esteemed in the quarters. Old men and women with great stores of riddles, proverbs, and folktales played a crucial role in teaching morality and training the youth to solve problems and to develop their memories. These cultural forms were all the more important because many of them came directly from Africa. Told by African-born slaves to their grandchildren, the ancient lore retained many of the motifs, structures, elaborate innuendoes, and much of the figurative speech characteristic of the originals. Probably about half of the lore was born out of the crucible of slavery and can be attributed to unknown individual creators. The riddle and the tale were the most important educational tools. Since a youngster's status among his peers was partially dependent on how accurately he recounted a tale or riddle he had heard from his elders, he early learned the importance of memorizing details. This early memory training is, I believe, the key to the remarkable accuracy of the memoirs of illiterate blacks so characteristic of the slave interviews and narratives and recently illustrated anew by Nate Shaw in *All God's Dangers*.

Since propounding and solving riddles involved both reasoning from the known to the unknown and answering deep philosophical questions, this practice was the central factor in the slave's development of analytical skills. Anyone examining slave riddles will find it easier to understand the seemingly amazing philosophical bent and impressive analyses of a William Wells Brown, Frederick Douglass, or Nate Shaw.

Literate slaves had even more status than those who taught by

resort to proverb, tale, and riddle, because they could read the
Bible, tell the bondsmen what was transpiring in the newspapers,
and write letters and passes. Many slaves and former bondsmen
have discussed the status of the literate slave in the quarters. A
fugitive slave in Canada declared in 1863 that among the slaves
there were some "who can read and write some, and of course
their influence will bear upon the others." One of these literate
bondsmen, John Sella Martin, reported that his ability to read
books and newspapers to Georgia slaves "elevated me to the
judgment seat of a second young Daniel among them."

Among the slaves accorded the highest status in the quarters
was the rebel, i.e., the bondsman who resisted floggings, violated
the racial taboos, or who ran away from the plantation. Described
as "high blooded" or "bad niggers" by their admirers, these
bondsmen found a central place in slave lore and songs. One
indication of the rebel's status was that antebellum blacks often
dated important events in their lives in relationship to Nat
Turner's insurrection. Almost universally, fugitive slaves found
aid in the quarters. The blacks spoke with pride of slaves who were
so intractable that they frightened whites. An Alabama bondswoman reported, "Dere wuz lot'ta mean 'niggers' in dem days too.
Some 'Niggers' so mean dat white fo'ks didn't bodder 'em much.
Ever' body knowed dey wuz mean. Will Marks wuz a bad 'Nigger'. . . . White fo'ks jes' scaid o' him . . . . Ma' marster use'ta
talk 'bout killin' im an' Miss Ann tell 'im 'You bedder not put your
hands on dat 'Nigger,' he kill ya.' "

There were a number of general things which contributed to
slave status. These included the possession of attractive clothes,
skill in making garden plots bloom, physical strength, ability to
read signs about the weather and to interpret dreams, and providing adequately for one's family. Age gradations represent one of
the keys to social structure with elders being viewed as the posses-
sors of wisdom, the closest link to the African homeland, and
persons to be treated with respect. A slave child who insulted an

old person was usually punished by that person and then later punished by his parents.

If, as scholars recognize in studying all other groups, slaves themselves ranked their fellows, we must discard the traditional characterization of slave social structure in favor of an in-group derived schema. The tentative suggestions made above represent one alternative way of viewing status in the quarters. Slave social structure was the most fluid in antebellum America. Since a slave had a 50/50 chance of being sold by the time he or she was fifty years old, the membership of every associational group changed constantly. A Protestant slave who enjoyed great status in the Upper South for piety might lose it forever, for instance, by being sold to Catholic Louisiana. Being under the control of the master, the slave's occupation often changed quickly. Besides this, most slaves were jacks-of-all-trades with "servants" and "artisans" often doing field labor. It was the rare large plantation where the division of labor was so rigid that a slave man or woman spent a lifetime working at one job. Or, as the slaves expressed it in one of their proverbs: "Tomorrow may be the carriage driver's day for plowing." Assuming that most of the observations made above are correct, the slave's valuation of roles can be represented by dividing the bondsmen into three classes:

A. Upper Class
1. Conjurors
2. Physicians and midwives
3. Preachers
4. Elders
5. Teachers
6. Creators and carriers of culture
7. Entertainers
8. Rebels

B. Middle Class
1. Creators of material culture
2. Verbal artists
3. Cool cats

4. Self-employed slaves
5. Bondsmen whose jobs frequently carried them away from the plantation
6. Artisans who made the slave's shoes, liquor, clothes, and houses
7. Artisans who made the slave's tools (blacksmiths, coopers)
8. Unusually strong, handsome, pretty, or intelligent field hands
9. Drivers who protected the slave's interests

C. Lower Class
1. Temporary house servants and servants residing in the quarters
2. Ordinary field hands
3. Exploitive drivers
4. Live-in house servants with long tenure
5. Voluntary concubines
6. Informants

This model varied, of course, from one plantation to another. It has little applicability to urban slaves. The rankings, after the small elite, are least precise within classes. But whatever its shortcomings, the model stresses the internal nature of the slave's social structure. When viewed in this way it is obvious that occupation represented only one among a multitude of status-creating factors. Only when a slave identified completely with his master's interest did he rank his fellows primarily on where they fitted into the plantation's occupational hierarchy. Like most other oppressed men and women, slaves did not depend solely for their prestige and status on the limited number of jobs open to them. If the slave could have aspired to the same range of jobs open to his master, then he might have placed as much stress on the prestige of occupations as did his white oppressors. The differences in the social structure of the oppressed and the oppressors continued into the twentieth century. And American blacks will continue to have a different social structure as long as they are an oppressed minority denied access to the places of power and prestige normally open to whites.

Slavery—The Historian's Burden

KENNETH M. STAMPP

Historians who study the slave experience in America always confront two traditional interpretations inherited from the nineteenth century. The first is a passionate indictment of slavery, the second an equally passionate defense. The roots of these traditions run back to the eighteenth century and especially to the Revolutionary generation. Therefore, in concluding our attempt at a bicentennial perspective, I find it both appropriate and necessary briefly to review the significance of the American Revolution in the history of slavery.

By 1776 slavery had existed in the English North American colonies for some 150 years; it was then not only firmly established as a practical labor system but clearly defined as an institution based on race—an institution suitable, or at the very least temporarily tolerable, for black people but not for white. Slavery survived the Revolution and was destined to thrive for another eighty years. In spite of an old myth that black bondage in the late eighteenth century was a weak and declining institution, historians have known for some time that it was instead both vital and profitable. "The years of slavery's supposed decline," Robert McColley reminds us, "were in fact the years of its greatest expansion." Even in Virginia the close of the four decades between 1776 and 1815 found slavery "fixed more securely" in the state's economy than it was at the start.[1]

Since the Revolution brought freedom to relatively few slaves,

A few paragraphs in this essay were first published in Paul David, et al., Reckoning with Slavery (Oxford University Press, 1976). They are included here with the permission of Oxford University Press.

one might easily conclude that for black Americans it had little immediate significance. For this reason some view the Revolutionary era as a time of lost opportunity, and the lost opportunity as a tragedy whose dimensions grew with each passing decade. Long before 1776, American churches had acknowledged the humanity of black people, had recognized that people of all races—whatever their differences—were equal in the sight of God, and had accepted responsibility for the conversion and salvation of the slaves. If this did not of itself make emancipation imperative, it at least made slaveholding morally risky, and the ideology of the Revolution compounded the risk. According to Winthrop Jordan, "it was perfectly clear that the principles for which Americans had fought required the complete abolition of slavery; the question was not *if* but *when* and *how*." Unfortunately, the answer to *when* was *not now*, and the opportunity was lost. "In retrospect," Jordan concludes, "the pity of antislavery's failure was that in the decade after the Revolution, success against slavery . . . seemed almost within reach. If the Negro had been freed in the late eighteenth century . . . he would have suffered far less degradation. . . . He would have undergone a shorter period of association with a radically debased status." Most important in Jordan's view, a general emancipation induced by the Revolution "would have been more than an improvised weapon in a fratricidal war. It would have come as a glorious triumph, the capstone of the Revolution . . . and the whole nation [would have] stirred with pride."[2] To this I would only add that emancipation at that time would have occurred under the best possible circumstances, for it would of necessity have been initiated by the southern states themselves. Emancipation would have been an extremely farsighted and quite extraordinary act of statesmanship, and would have been justly celebrated as the most momentous event of the Revolution.

If hindsight reveals the lost opportunity and the ultimate tragedy, it also forces us to acknowledge the formidable obstacles in the way of emancipation—slavery's great economic strength, the weakness of the southern emancipationists, the near universality of racial prejudice North and South, and the loopholes in Revolutionary ideology that permitted a subversion of the spirit of the Declaration of Independence.[3] However, these obstacles by no means undermine Professor Jordan's case for a lost opportunity or lessen the dimensions of the tragedy it entailed. As difficult as emancipation would have been in 1776, it would always be more difficult thereafter. If in 1776 slavery had great economic strength, in 1860 it was stronger still; if southern emancipationists of the Revolutionary generation were weak, it was their fate henceforth to grow weaker. If racial prejudice was rampant in the eighteenth century, it was bolstered by a systematic body of racial thought in the nineteenth; if there were loopholes in the ideology of liberty and equality during the Revolution, in later years proslavery radicals rejected the principles of the Declaration of Independence altogether. In short, no time was as propitious for emancipation by state action as the time of the Revolution—never thereafter could it have been accomplished with less pain, however painful it would have been even then.

Though we must think of the Revolution, in part, as a time of lost opportunity, we must not overlook what was accomplished and what at least was begun. In no previous generation did as many whites, for religious or secular reasons, have doubts about the morality of slavery; never before had there been such an outpouring of antislavery tracts. This moral concern was one reason among several why all the states soon closed the African slave trade,[4] why the northern states—where the slave interest was relatively small—adopted plans of gradual emancipation, and why Congress in 1787 prohibited slavery in the Northwest Territory. In the South the slave interest was very strong, but few cared then to contend that slavery was a positive good; and many found comfort in a belief that one day slavery would give way to an inexorable and benevolent progress.

On matters relating to slavery the Quakers of the Revolutionary generation became the custodians of the American conscience. In 1774, the Philadelphia Yearly Meeting, having previously urged Quaker masters to prepare their slaves for freedom, required its members to emancipate them. In 1776, that body instructed local meetings to disown those who refused. Maryland Quakers adopted a similar policy in 1778, Virginia Quakers in 1784. Both the Pennsylvania Abolition Society and the New York Manumission Society, formed in the 1780s, were dominated by Quakers.[5] In this manner, slavery for the first time became the target of organized groups seeking its eradication; in the long run this action by men of the Revolutionary generation, however small their number, was the most fateful of all. In 1790, Pennsylvania Quakers and the Pennsylvania Abolition Society petitioned Congress to use its power to advance the cause of emancipation. The resulting angry debate was the first of many that troubled national politics during the next seven decades—debates which evoked every conceivable argument to defend or attack the economic efficiency, social arrangements, and personal relationships of a slave society.

Thus we must turn to the Revolutionary generation to find the first substantial concern about the morality and social consequences of slavery, as well as the beginnings of institutional attacks and of the demand for political action. From the controversies they generated in legislative halls, church bodies, social organizations, newspapers, periodicals, and tracts came the earliest formulations of what eventually became the two traditional interpretations of slavery—interpretations that reached their full fruition as systematic arguments during the nineteenth-century sectional conflict. One of these traditional interpretations was ultimately associated with the antebellum northern abolitionist movement, the other with the antebellum southern defense of slavery. Both of them have had an enduring impact on American thought, not only about slavery but about the place of black people in American society. They have even affected the work of twentieth-century historians, for everyone who has written about slavery in some degree betrays his debt to, or feels compelled to quarrel with, one or the other of these traditional interpretations.

Robert W. Fogel and Stanley Engerman, in their recent book *Time on the Cross*, describe and criticize such an interpretation—which they call *the* traditional interpretation, as if it were the only one of consequence in the historiography of slavery. *The* traditional interpretation described by Fogel and Engerman consists of five fundamental generalizations: (1) that, except on new land, capital investments in slaves were generally unprofitable, unless the owner supplied surplus slaves to the interstate slave trade; (2) that slavery in the late antebellum period was a dying institution; (3) that slave labor and the agricultural economy that exploited it were "economically inefficient"; (4) that slavery produced a stagnant, or retarded, southern economy; and (5) "that slavery provided extremely harsh material conditions of life for the typical slave."[6]

However, what Fogel and Engerman identify as *the* traditional interpretation of slavery is in the main simply the old abolitionist interpretation. Abolitionist propaganda emphasized (and doubtless exaggerated) cruelties, atrocities, and harsh material conditions of life for the purpose of winning converts. Tales of slaves who died of overwork, physical neglect, or brutal punishment, stories of broken families and sexual exploitation filled the speeches and tracts of these ardent crusaders. Their interpretation of slavery was, after all, a case for the prosecution, not the cool, balanced, detached judgment of which modern historians fancy they are capable. Although abolitionists showed relatively little interest in the economics of slavery, their occasional comments indicated a conviction that the southern economy was backward, that capital investments in slaves were unprofitable, and that slave labor was inefficient.

In its refutation of *the* traditional interpretation of slavery, *Time on the Cross* claims to offer "a wide-ranging and radical reinterpretation." The major points of this reinterpretation are: (1) that slavery was a rational labor system which survived because it was profitable; (2) that on the eve of the Civil War slavery was still flourishing and gave no indication of an imminent collapse for economic reasons; (3) that slave agriculture was efficient and the slave field hand typically a diligent laborer; (4) that the southern economy, far from being backward, was characterized by rapid growth; and (5) that the slave system was not harsh but benign, protecting slave family life, avoiding sexual exploitation, preferring positive labor incentives to physical punishment, and providing a standard of living which "compared favorably with [that] . . . of free industrial workers."[7]

The remarkable feature of this "radical reinterpretation" is that it is, in its essential points, largely a recapitulation of the *second* traditional interpretation of slavery—the interpretation developed by southern proslavery writers. This second tradition, like *Time on the Cross*, stresses mild treatment, moderate discipline, wholesome and comfortable living conditions, stable family life, and minimal sexual exploitation. Proslavery writers attributed the alleged generally good treatment of slaves partly to the master's benevolence and partly to his self-interest as a practical businessman. "When slaves are worth near a thousand dollars a head," argued George Fitzhugh, "they will be carefully and well provided for."[8] Thomas R. Dew, professor of history, metaphysics, and political law at William and Mary College, was the first southerner to develop this line of argument in an extended and systematic essay.[9] In fact, Dew's 1832 essay, though borrowing heavily from earlier writers, was probably the first booklength defense of slavery ever written anywhere. If I were to locate *Time on the Cross* in the historiography of slavery, I would identify it with this second traditional interpretation; if I were looking for a label, I would be tempted to call it Neo-Dewism. Needless to say, the book is not a defense of slavery, and its argument is not racist as was Dew's; but its highly favorable assessment of life in bondage nonetheless originated in the traditional proslavery interpretation. Even the economic argument in *Time on the Cross* concerning the rationality, profitability, and viability of slavery, the efficiency of slave agriculture, and the relative wealth and prosperity of the antebellum South might be labeled, without undue exaggeration, Neo-Dewism. Proslavery writers, like the abolitionists, paid relatively little attention to the economics of slavery. A few, when they did address the problem, conceded to their northern critics that free labor was cheaper and more efficient and defended their system in other ways. More often they advanced an economic defense as well. Dew argued that the profitability of slave labor was proven by the fact that it existed; had it not been profitable, it would have been abolished. In Virginia, he claimed, slave labor "gives value to her soil . . . ; take away this, and you pull down the atlas that upholds the whole system."[10] Thornton Stringfellow presented evidence that the five Atlantic slave states during the previous two hundred years had accumulated substantially greater wealth than the New England states. Therefore, he asked, "Is it possible . . . to believe that slavery tends to poverty[?]" On the contrary, he contended, "slavery, as an agricultural investment, is more profitable than an investment in commerce and manufactures."[11]

Thus it is plausible to argue that Fogel and Engerman do not so much destroy a traditional interpretation of slavery as elaborate on and reinforce one whose source runs back to southern proslavery writers. Of course, to label them Neo-Dewists does not of itself discredit their elaborate argument, any more than labeling other historians of slavery Neo-Abolitionists discredits theirs. Indeed, there is danger in all labels of this sort, for they may lead to a kind of reductionism that blurs rather than clarifies the various perspectives from which historians have written about American slavery. No twentieth-century historian of slavery subscribes to the five fundamental generalizations that constitute *the* traditional interpretation described in *Time on the Cross*. The authors identify none who do; they merely claim that this tradition is incorporated in a "vast literature" written by "hundreds of historians" and "taught in most high school and college classes across the nation."[12] No twentieth-century historian is a consistent Neo-Abolitionist; none is a consistent Neo-Dewist—not even, to be quite honest, Fogel and Engerman.

The most durable tradition of historians of slavery, like that of all American historians, is revisionism—the ceaseless testing and challenging of old interpretations, and the rewriting of history in the light of new data, new methodologies, new perceptions of human behavior, and new perspectives. I am not sure that revisionism always represents progress—we all like some revisions better than others—but it is what keeps our profession alive and gives excitement to teaching and research. In their day the writings of Ulrich B. Phillips on slavery were both highly original and decidedly revisionist. They conform to neither the traditional interpretation described in *Time on the Cross*, which is Neo-Abolitionism, nor in all respects to Neo-Dewism. Rather, Phillips' portrayal of slavery draws on the economic arguments of its critics and, to some extent, on the racial and sociological arguments of its defenders. Each of his successors has offered a new synthesis, parts of which can be traced back to one or the other of the two traditions, but none of which can be easily labeled or pigeonholed. *Time on the Cross* contains some passionate passages that would have outraged Thomas R. Dew and George Fitzhugh. Eugene Genovese's recent book on slavery, *Roll, Jordan, Roll*,[13] defies all attempts at labeling and classification. Calling slavery a crime, as he does in his preface, would hardly have endeared him to pro-slavery writers; discovering "solid virtues" in slaveholders, as he does throughout his book, would have turned off most abolitionists; and, in spite of his use of some Marxist concepts and categories, his book as a whole is well calculated to drive any true and consistent Marxist out of his mind.

For almost three quarters of a century, since Phillips launched his seminal work, slavery has been the historians' burden. What the specialists have to say about the peculiar institution eventually finds its way into secondary and college level textbooks and thus makes a significant impact on what black and white Americans think of their past, of themselves, and of each other. Never were as many historians concerned about slavery as a historical problem as today. In no previous decade were as many books and articles published on the subject as in the last; and, I am sorry to say, never were historians farther away from a consensus on major problems than now. Of all the issues relating to slavery that historians have debated in recent years, I can think of only one toward which they seem to be reaching general agreement—the profitability of exploiting slave labor in the antebellum South. Today few would challenge the assertion in *Time on the Cross* that "slavery was not a system irrationally kept in existence by plantation owners who failed to perceive or were indifferent to their best economic interests. The purchase of a slave was generally a highly profitable investment."[14] Until recently Eugene Genovese was one of the more vigorous dissenters, contending that slavery was relatively unprofitable, or at least tended toward unprofitability. The problem is not particularly relevant to the subjects of his last two books, but in *Roll, Jordan, Roll* he does hint that the conflict may be over with a brief observation that slaveholders "profited from an evil social system."[15]

If the dispute over profitability has subsided, nearly every other question about the southern slave economy is presently the subject of lively disagreement. Nothing approaching a consensus exists among scholars on whether the antebellum South was characterized by slow or rapid economic growth, whether the future of slavery in 1860 was bright or dim, whether slave agriculture was more or less efficient than northern free farms, and whether slave field hands worked more or less diligently than their white counterparts. *Time on the Cross* seems only to have intensified the debate, for numerous historians have expressed dissatisfaction with both its methods and conclusions.[16] Perhaps conventional historians would be well advised to leave these questions to the so-called "new economic historians" and their cliometric procedures. Since none of the southern plantations was operated with free labor, determining the comparative efficiency of slave agriculture and the diligence of field hands is at best a tricky business. In any case, while conventional historians await the outcome of this war of the computers, there are numerous problems whose exploration are better suited to their methodology.

The nature of the antebellum slaveholding class has not yet been settled, the principal protagonists at present being Genovese on one side and Fogel and Engerman on the other. In Genovese's view the slaveholders developed a unique culture whose values were essentially prebourgeois, stressing "a patriarchal and paternalistic ethos."[17] Fogel and Engerman portray the planters as hard-headed, practical entrepreneurs whose goals were efficiency and maximum profits. Several issues are involved in this controversy, but none is more crucial than whether the planters were exceptionally prone to dissipate their income in various forms of conspicuous consumption. Did they as a class show a contempt for thrift? Did they, more than other classes with comparable incomes, squander their earnings on expensive houses, long holidays, fine wines, armies of servants, lavish entertainments, and other luxuries? Of course, the generous hospitality and high standard of living of antebellum planters are proverbial, but some time ago Stanley Engerman expressed doubt that conspicuous consumption in the South exceeded that in the North. He notes that affluent northerners also built mansions and indulged in other forms of "what, from the point of view of economic growth, may be called social waste." Moreover, Engerman reminds us, "If you ask of the South: 'What is the maximum amount of capital formation which could have occurred in the absence of conspicuous consumption?' and don't ask that question about the North, you will get a rather misleading answer."[18] Jane H. Pease accurately observes that no historian has ever tested the validity of our traditional notions about southern consumption patterns, adding, "The evidence for greater Southern than Northern waste of potential savings for personal indulgence has never been presented."[19]

This being the case, a comparative study of the values and of the spending and saving habits of southern planters and northern businessmen is long overdue. I suspect that such a study will reverse the traditional picture, and we will find that when northern business families and southern planter families had enjoyed wealth for approximately equal lengths of time, the northerners spent relatively more on luxuries than the southerners. I suspect this, first, because I doubt that the values of the two classes were significantly different; and, second, because the northern urban business classes had greater opportunities and were under greater pressure to indulge in luxuries than the isolated rural southern planters. A single northern case will hardly settle this issue, but a good place to begin is with the published diary of George Templeton Strong, a wealthy and urbane New York lawyer.[20] Strong's diary records his immense taste for the social and cultural amenities of his city and makes one at least want to withhold judgment about the planters until the results of a thorough comparative study are available.

However fascinating the problems relating to the economics of slavery and the nature of the planter class, none can be of more fundamental importance than those that concern the slaves themselves. Here again historians are locked in controversy over a wide range of issues, including some that one might have expected to be settled empirically long ago. Debates reminiscent of those between the abolitionists and the Dewists rage over how well slaves were housed, fed, and clothed, what kind of medical care they received, how hard they were worked, how severely they were punished, what proportion of them became victims of the interstate slave trade, whether most slave children grew up in stable, nuclear families, and how frequently slave women were exploited sexually. Some of these questions can be dealt with fruitfully by the quantitative methods of the social scientists; others, because of the nature of the evidence, can be handled best by conventional historians experienced in the critical use of literary sources. All of them are of an order that permits some sort of reasonable and persuasive resolution. Though historians have not yet resolved the argument, there is no reason why questions relating to the slave's standard of living cannot be settled as successfully as the question of slavery's profitability. Perhaps out of the present debate between Fogel and Engerman and their critics agreement on at least some of these questions may be reached.

A far more challenging order of problems concerns the impact of bondage on the minds and personalities of the slaves. No historian has been content to stop with estimates of their standard of living and physical treatment; in varying degrees all have ventured to interpret the subjective and unmeasurable data relating to slave culture, the sources, metaphysics, and significance of slave religion, the role of slave families, the interaction of masters and slaves, and the psychology of slave behavior, including accommodation, submission, and resistance.

Over these complex and elusive problems, all of them freighted with moral implications and nearly inseparable from ideological commitments, historians have disagreed with extraordinary passion. They are nowhere near a consensus on any of them, and they may never be. For example, consider the following two sets of hypotheses and counterhypotheses from the books of four historians. Ulrich B. Phillips argues that, "In the main the American Negroes . . . were more or less contentedly slaves, with grievances from time to time but not ambition. . . . [They] lived in each moment as it flew, and left 'Old Massa' to take such thought as the morrow might need." However, Herbert Aptheker counters with the generalization that "discontent and rebelliousness were not only exceedingly common, but, indeed, characteristic of American Negro slaves." Stanley Elkins claims that the slave's "relationship with his master was one of utter dependence and childlike attachment; it was indeed this childlike quality that was the very key to his being." But John Blassingame contends that the typical field hand "was sullenly obedient and hostilely submissive. . . . The docility of the slave was a sham, a mask to hide his true feelings and personality traits."[21]

These statements illustrate the striking variety of historical perceptions of the slave's personality and mind. But their authors have one thing in common—all four of them argue beyond their evidence (as do Fogel and Engerman, Genovese, and Stampp) when they touch on matters as nearly impenetrable as these. All of them make generalizations about the character of slaves that are to a significant degree unproved and perhaps unprovable— generalizations that can be defended, if at all, only as plausible explanations for a limited and inconclusive amount of data. To understand fully the perceptions of each historian on these highly subjective questions one must understand the historian himself, for each of his impressionistic generalizations is a segment of a broader conceptualization that he has imposed on fragmentary evidence.

The reason that historians tend to argue beyond their evidence is that they demand answers to questions about slave life for which the available evidence is hopelessly inadequate. None of us really wants to admit that the answers to some questions may lie permanently beyond our reach no matter how diligent our research, how ingenious our methods, and how imaginative our conceptualizations. But consider what the historian is up against when he tries to determine what the slave felt and thought about his bondage, or what his religious experiences were, or what the quality of his family life was. Most of the conventional literary sources for information of this kind simply do not exist. The slaves had no organizations, no literary or political spokesmen, and no newspapers; they kept no diaries and rarely wrote letters. We are indebted to Robert Starobin for collecting and publishing the few letters from slaves that survive; but since most of them were written to white masters and mistresses, they do not help us penetrate very deeply into the mind of the slave.[22] No congressional committee investigated the conditions of American slavery or permitted slaves to give their own testimony. No antebellum oral history project collected data through the systematic interviewing of slaves. The evidence from white slaveholders about the lives of slaves is immense—some of it of great value—but the evidence from the slaves themselves is but a small trickle.

Slave evidence in twentieth-century historical writings comes chiefly in three forms—the autobiographies of fugitives, slave narratives based on oral interviews undertaken in the 1920s and 1930s, and postbellum collections of slave songs and folklore. These sources have been exploited extensively—too often uncritically, as if they were the long-lost keys to a full understanding of the slave's mind, feelings, and personality. I do not mean to suggest that they have no value, but I do think that their extensive use merely illustrates the scarcity of good source material and the desperation of historians who strive to understand slave life.[23] In evaluating the quality of this material, we should remember that slaveholders also wrote autobiographies; but historians use them cautiously and sparingly, because the diaries, letters, and other contemporary writings of slaveholders are plentiful and vastly superior as sources. For the same reason, no one in the 1930s belatedly proposed a program to interview former slaveholders.

Slave autobiographies and narratives hardly inspire confidence in their reliability when they are subjected to the tests that should be used in evaluating all forms of historical evidence. For example, historians, like courts of law, are highly skeptical of secondhand or hearsay evidence. Therefore it is important to know that most of the autobiographies of former slaves were actually written by white amanuenses. In an autobiography of this kind we never hear directly from the former slave; instead we read what a white author tells us in *his* words a former slave told him. I do not propose that we reject altogether this hearsay evidence—we cannot be quite as rigid as courts of law—only that we use it with extreme caution and with a clear understanding of what it is.

Historians, again like courts of law, agree that the best evidence is not only firsthand but recorded soon after the event. This rule is especially relevant to the evaluation of slave narratives compiled in the 1920s and 1930s.[24] These narratives were given to us by people who were, on the average, more than eighty-five-years-old, who were born in the 1850s, and who were children when the Civil War began. For the slave experience all we can obtain from them are the memories of childhood after the passage of more than seventy years.

Finally, the historian must always consider the circumstances which produced a body of evidence and the motives of those who provided it. We properly discount as special pleading the public defenses of slavery written by slaveholders; but we must also take account of the extremely subjective influences that helped to shape the autobiographies and narratives of former slaves. It is not enough merely to say that *all* sources are biased, or that historians have methods for dealing with the problem of bias, for these autobiographies and narratives present some rather special problems. In addition to the common shortcomings of auto-biographies—special pleading, the author's desire to make himself look heroic or long-suffering, and above all, his fallible and selective memory—those of former slaves were usually tailored to the tastes of a northern antislavery audience. Even some of the best of them, including the autobiography of Frederick Douglass written by himself, were in part abolitionist tracts. The slave narratives of the 1930s were gathered by predominantly white interviewers at a time when race relations in the rural South hardly encouraged candor. The narrators were not only very old but characteristically very poor and economically dependent on whites. Many of them seemed to believe that the interview might have some bearing on their chances of receiving a rumored federal pension. The importance of these subjective influences can be illustrated by the following facts—slavery was remembered as a harsh institution by 7 percent of the narrators interviewed by whites and by 25 percent of those interviewed by blacks, by 16 percent of the narrators living in the South and by 38 percent of those living in the North, by 3 percent of the narrators clearly dependent on white support and by 23 percent of those who seemed to be financially independent. Comparing the nineteenth-century autobiographies of former slaves with the narratives of the 1930s, the autobiographies describe life in bondage decidedly less favorably than the narratives. Given the very different external pressures on the autobiographers and narrators, this result is hardly surprising.[25]

Another source of direct evidence concerning the minds and personalities of slaves has not yet been fully exploited, but it may prove to be the most valuable of all. This is the evidence provided by the freedmen in the years immediately following their liberation, perhaps until the end of the 1860s. The time of emancipation was a crucial point in the history of black people in America—a "moment of truth," as Eugene Genovese calls it. When four million slaves were transformed into freedmen they found opportunities that had never existed before to explain in their own words who they were and what they thought. Their behavior, though still far from uninhibited, found its motivating force from within a good deal more than in slavery days, when so much of it had to conform to the norms set by white masters. In short, the 1860s was a time of self-revelation, a time when the testimony of those who had lived in slavery first became a significant part of the historical record.

Of course, all freedmen did not suddenly find voices or begin an orgy of letter-writing and diary-keeping—after all, well over 90 percent of them were illiterate. Nevertheless they did speak in unprecedented numbers. They expressed their opinions to members of the freedmen's aid societies and to agents of the Freedmen's Bureau; some of them even testified before congressional committees. Very soon black newspapers appeared in the South, and their editors began to get some input from the freedmen themselves. Leaders emerged from their ranks to speak for them; within a few years some served in constitutional conventions, in state legislatures, and a small handful in Congress. More than ever before, the masses of blacks moved about freely, consulted their own wishes and interests, and made their own decisions. For the first time those who had been slaves could come together in religious and secular organizations that they controlled. The crucial fact about all these developments is that they occurred when it was still possible to study the freedmen in action with the minds and personalities that had been formed in slavery days. Thus, compared to the limited testimony available from earlier years, we have during the 1860s a veritable explosion of firsthand testimony from those who so very recently had been slaves. Here, surely, is some of the best evidence historians can hope to find to answer the questions they have been asking about the culture, personalities, and minds of black people in bondage. Eugene Genovese, Benjamin Quarles, Willie Lee Rose, Vernon Lane Wharton, and Joel Williamson, among others, have already exploited this evidence in their writings, but I think that this "moment of truth" or of self-revelation requires a full-scale study of its own.

These, then, are the black sources for nearly all we are able to learn directly about the mind of the slave. They tell us much, though far less than we would like to know—and too often pretend to know. However, for the *external* behavior of slaves, from which historians can draw inferences, speculate, and hypothesize about the slave mind and personality, three kinds of white sources exist which I think are at least as valuable as the available black sources. These consist of the diaries of slaveholders, the essays written by slaveholders on the management of slaves, and the advertisements for fugitive slaves. I am not suggesting that they can tell us anything directly about what slaves thought or felt; but as sources for the behavior of slaves, I do think that they pass the tests for the evaluation of historical evidence remarkably well. First, all of them provide large quantities of firsthand rather than hearsay evidence; second, they record events soon after they occurred;

last, external pressures for distortion were minimal, while internal pressures to report accurately were substantial. Slaveholders kept diaries for their own private use, not for public consumption. Although we must be aware of the unconscious censorship that may affect the contents of even a private diary, historians justly prize these documents as among the most candid sources available to them. Slaveholders' essays on slave management were published in southern agricultural periodicals that circulated mostly among the slaveholders themselves. Their purpose was not propagandistic but to offer professional advice. We must, of course, make allowances for the inclination of the writers to establish a good image among their peers; but my impression of these essays is that they are, by and large, remarkably candid about the problems of managing slaves and are rich in illustrative details. In the advertisements for fugitive slaves, which deserve more attention than they have received, the major exception to their descriptive reliability is the frequent insistence of the master that his slave ran away for "no cause." But to misrepresent the appearance or characteristic behavior of a fugitive would obviously defeat the purpose of advertising. Therefore, historians interested in the slave's culture and in what can be inferred about his mind and personality from his behavior should not overlook the evidence available in these white sources.

In the past, historians have written about the interior life of the slave from a variety of perspectives. Given the problem of sources, interpretations are likely to be as various in the future. At the conclusion of *Roll, Jordan, Roll*, Eugene Genovese makes a statement that every historian of slavery would be well advised to make. He offers his reading of the sources as "one historian's considered judgment," and he warns nonspecialists that "all the sources are treacherous and that no 'definitive' study has been or ever will be written." Perhaps one could say that about all written history, but it is especially fitting to say it about the writings on a subject for which the sources are so distressingly obscure.

Notes

Notes to THE SOUTHERN SLAVE ECONOMY
by Stanley L. Engerman

1. This paper is an unrevised version of my presentation at the symposium. For this reason, and because I have discussed similar issues in several of the publications cited below, I have attempted to hold footnotes to a bare minimum, using them only when some source citation seemed necessary. Since this paper was not intended to serve as a response to critics, even though I do deal with several issues which are being discussed, it seemed inappropriate to cite that literature except when used for necessary substantive information. Research underlying this discussion has been financed by the National Science Foundation.

2. Albert Fishlow, "Antebellum Interregional Trade Reconsidered," *American Economic Review*, LIV (May, 1964), 352–64, places the share at 23 percent of income in 1839 and 29 percent in 1860.

3. These estimates are based upon calculations allocating the Towne–Rasmussen agricultural output estimates for that year among regions based upon shares of livestock and crop output as reported in the census. See Marvin W. Towne and Wayne D. Rasmussen, "Farm Gross Product and Gross Investment in the Nineteenth Century," in Conference on Research in Income and Wealth, *Trends in the American Economy in the Nineteenth Century*, Studies in Income and Wealth, Vol. 24 (Princeton, 1960), 255–312, and U.S. Census Office, Seventh (1850) *Seventh Census of the United States*, (Washington, 1853), lxxxii–lxxxiii.

4. Lewis Cecil Gray, *History of Agriculture in the Southern United States To 1860* (Washington, 1933), 530–31.

5. *Ibid.*, 482, 483, 530.

6. Philip D. Curtin, *The Atlantic Slave Trade*, (Madison, 1969), 268; Robert William Fogel and Stanley L. Engerman, *Time on the Cross, Vol. 1: The Economics of American Negro Slavery; Vol. 2: Evidence and Methods* (Boston, 1974), I, 28.

7. Robert S. Starobin, *Industrial Slavery in the Old South* (New York, 1970); Fred Bateman, James Foust, and Thomas Weiss, "Profitability in Southern Manufacturing: Estimates for 1860," *Explorations in Economic History*, XII (July, 1975), 211–31; Charles B. Dew, "Disciplining Slave Ironworkers in the Antebellum South: Coercion, Conciliation, and Accommodation," *American Historical Review*, LXXIX (April, 1974), 393–418.

172 Notes

8. Douglass C. North, *The Economic Growth of the United States, 1790–1860* (Englewood Cliffs, 1961); Fishlow, "Antebellum Interregional Trade Reconsidered"; Stanley L. Engerman, "The Antebellum South: What Probably Was and What Should Have Been," *Agricultural History*, XLIV (January, 1970), 127–42; and Lawrence A. Herbst, "Interregional Commodity Trade from the North to the South and American Economic Development in the Antebellum Period" (Ph.D. dissertation, University of Pennsylvania, 1974).

9. J. D. B. DeBow, *The Industrial Resources, Statistics, &c. of the United States, and more particularly of the Southern and Western States* (New York, 1854), II, 313–15.

10. George Tucker, *Progress of the United States in Population and Wealth in Fifty Years* (New York, 1855), 108–18.

11. Alfred H. Conrad and John R. Meyer, "The Economics of Slavery in the Ante Bellum South," *Journal of Political Economy*, LXVI (April, 1958), 95–130.

12. Gavin Wright, "Slavery and the Cotton Boom," *Explorations in Economic History*, XII (October, 1975), 439–51.

13. For an excellent study of economic aspects of the slave plantation, see Ralph V. Anderson, "Labor Utilization and Productivity, Diversification and Self Sufficiency, Southern Plantations, 1800–1840" (Ph.D. dissertation, University of North Carolina, Chapel Hill, 1974). Also see Claudia Dale Goldin, *Urban Slavery in the American South, 1820–1860* (Chicago, 1976).

14. David Hume, "Of the Populousness of Ancient Nations," in Eugene Rotwein (ed.), *David Hume—Writings on Economics* (Madison, 1955), 119.

15. Stanley M. Elkins, *Slavery* (Chicago, 1959), 37–80; Richard Sutch, "The Breeding of Slaves for Sale and the Westward Expansion of Slavery, 1850–1860," in Stanley L. Engerman and Eugene D. Genovese (eds.), *Race and Slavery in the Western Hemisphere: Quantitative Studies* (Princeton, 1975), 173–210.

16. It should be made clear that the numbers here are hypothetical, and relative magnitudes are introduced only to place the use of quantitative measures in some interpretive context. The actual numbers are, of course, the subject of considerable debate among scholars.

17. For the latest discussion of these points see Stanley L. Engerman, "A Reconsideration of Southern Economic Growth, 1770–1860," *Agricultural History*, XLIX (April, 1975), 343–61, as well as the subsequent critique by Harold D. Woodman, "New Perspectives on Southern Economic Development: A Comment," *Agricultural History*, XLIX (April, 1975), 374–80. I am grateful to Woodman for comments on several papers, and have greatly benefited from his publications on this subject.

18. Roger Ransom and Richard Sutch, "The Impact of the Civil War and of Emancipation on Southern Agriculture," *Explorations in Economic History*, XII (January, 1975), 1–28.

19. Gavin Wright, "Cotton Competition and the Post-Bellum Recovery of the American South," *Journal of Economic History*, XXXIV (September, 1974), 610–35; Charles W. Ramsdell, "The Natural Limits of Slavery Expansion," *Mississippi Valley Historical Review*, XVI (September, 1929), 151–71.

20. Robert E. Gallman, "Trends in the Size Distribution of Wealth in the Nineteenth Century: Some Speculations," in Conference on Research in Income and Wealth, *Six Papers on the Size Distribution of Wealth and Income*, Studies in Income and Wealth, Vol. 33 (New York, 1969), 1–25; Lee Soltow, *Men and Wealth in the United States, 1850–1870* (New Haven, 1975).

21. See, for example, Robert E. Gallman, "Self-Sufficiency in the Cotton Economy of the Antebellum South," *Agricultural History*, XLIV (January, 1970), 5–23, and Engerman, "The Antebellum South."

22. David Brion Davis, *The Problem of Slavery in the Age of Revolution, 1770–1823* (Ithaca, 1975); Eric Foner, *Free Soil, Free Labor, Free Men* (New York, 1970).

23. Robert W. Fogel and Stanley L. Engerman, "The Relative Efficiency of Slavery: A Comparison of Northern and Southern Agriculture in 1860," *Explorations in Economic History*, VIII (Spring, 1971), 353–67.

24. Fogel and Engerman, *Time on the Cross*, I, 191–209; II, 126–152.

25. *Ibid.*, II, 135, 137; Fogel and Engerman, "The Relative Efficiency of Slavery." At the least, southern efficiency was 96 percent of northern, even on this extreme assumption as to price change and flexibility of adjustment.

26. Julius Rubin, "The Limits of Agricultural Progress in the Nineteenth-Century South," *Agricultural History*, XLIX (April, 1975), 362–73.

27. Fogel and Engerman, *Time on the Cross*, II, 139; Wright, "Slavery and the Cotton Boom"; Gavin Wright and Howard Kunreuther, "Cotton, Corn and Risk in the Nineteenth Century," *Journal of Economic History*, XXV (September, 1975), 526–51.

28. This is based on comparisons of the increased regional production of various crops between 1850 and 1860 as indicated in the respective Censuses of Agriculture.

29. For growth of cotton output see Towne and Rasmussen, "Farm Gross Product and Gross Investment in the Nineteenth Century," 308, and U.S. Bureau of the Census, *Historical Statistics of the United States* (Washington, 1961), 302.

30. See, for example, the estimates in Richard A. Easterlin, "Farm Production and Income in Old and New Areas at Mid-Century," in David C. Klingaman and Richard K. Vedder (eds.), *Essays in Nineteenth Century Economic History* (Athens, 1975), 77–117.

Notes to SLAVERY—THE WHITE MAN'S BURDEN
by William K. Scarborough

1. For a more extended discussion of the relationship between the civil rights movement and recent writings on slavery, see David Herbert Donald's review of *Roll, Jordan, Roll* in *Commentary* (January, 1975), 86.

2. Kenneth M. Stampp, *The Peculiar Institution: Slavery in the Ante-Bellum South* (New York: Alfred A. Knopf, 1956), 5.

3. William K. Scarborough (ed.), *The Diary of Edmund Ruffin*, 3 Vols. (Baton Rouge, 1972–), II, 604.

4. Morton Rothstein, "The Antebellum South as a Dual Economy: A Tentative Hypothesis," *Agricultural History*, XLI (October, 1967), 375–76.

5. Slave Inventories for 1851, Stephen Duncan Plantation, 1851–1861, Schedule of Estate, Stephen Duncan Plantation Journal, April 15, 1864, Duncan (Stephen and Stephen, Jr.) Papers, III, IV, V, Louisiana State University Department of Archives, Baton Rouge; Paul Wallace Gates, *The Farmer's Age: Agriculture, 1815–1860* (New York: Holt, Rinehart and Winston, 1960), 148, 407; Rothstein, "The Antebellum South as a Dual Economy," 378–81. For more on Duncan, see William K. Scarborough, "Heartland of the Cotton Kingdom," in R. A. McLemore (ed.), *A History of Mississippi*, 2 Vols. (Hattiesburg, 1973), I, 343–49.

174   Notes

6. Printed Obituary, July 4, 1887, in Duncan F. Kenner Papers, Louisiana State University Department of Archives.
7. Rothstein, "The Antebellum South as a Dual Economy," 379–81.
8. Robert W. Fogel and Stanley L. Engerman, *Time on the Cross: The Economics of American Negro Slavery* (Boston, 1974), 73.
9. Eugene D. Genovese, *Roll, Jordan, Roll: The World the Slaves Made* (New York, 1974).
10. John W. Blassingame, *The Slave Community: Plantation Life in the Antebellum South* (New York, 1972).
11. Scarborough (ed.), *Diary of Edmund Ruffin*, II, 209.
12. *De Bow's Review*, X (June, 1851), 622.
13. Maunsel White to Stillman, Allan & Company, December 1, 1845, Maunsel White Lettercopy Book, in Maunsel White Papers and Books, Southern Historical Collection, University of North Carolina, Chapel Hill.
14. For a concise summary of current opinion within the academic community concerning this controversial book, see Thomas L. Haskell, "The True & Tragical History of *Time on the Cross,*" *New York Review of Books*, XXII (October 2, 1975), 33–39.
15. Valcour Aime, *Plantation Diary* (New Orleans: Clark and Hofeline, 1878), 167; Solon Robinson, "Agricultural Tour South and West," *American Agriculturist*, VIII (November, 1849), 338; Bayside Plantation Records (MSS in Southern Historical Collection), I, November 19, 1848; January 20, 1850.
16. Magnolia Plantation Journals (MSS in Henry Clay Warmoth Papers and Books, Southern Historical Collection), October 4, 1858; White Hill Plantation Books (Microfilm copy in Southern Historical Collection), VI.
17. Deer Range Plantation Journal (Maunsel White Papers and Books), July 4, 1858; Franklin L. Riley (ed.), "Diary of a Mississippi Planter," *Publications of the Mississippi Historical Society* (Oxford, Miss., 1909), X, 356.
18. John Carmichael Jenkins Plantation Diary (Typescript in John C. Jenkins and Family Papers, Louisiana State University Department of Archives), December 25, 1847.
19. Joan Parker Caldwell, "Christmas in Old Natchez," *Journal of Mississippi History*, XXI (October, 1959), 257, 259–60, 269.
20. *Ibid.*, 261; Charles S. Sydnor, *A Gentleman of the Old Natchez Region: Benjamin L. C. Wailes* (Durham, 1938), 103–104.
21. Edwin A. Davis, *Plantation Life in the Florida Parishes of Louisiana, 1836–46, as Reflected in the Diary of Bennet H. Barrow* (New York, 1943), 218; size of slave force from MS census returns, 1840 (Microfilm copy in Louisiana State University Library, Baton Rouge), West Feliciana Parish, Louisiana.
22. Davis, *Plantation Life in Louisiana*, 279; Westover Plantation Journal (Microfilm copy in Southern Historical Collection), December 25, 1858; December 25, 1861.
23. For examples of planters who regularly purchased such items as corn, hay, and poultry from their Negroes, see Bayside Plantation Records (Southern Historical Collection); Aime, *Plantation Diary*, 58, 64, 77; James Hamilton Couper Plantation Records (MSS in Southern Historical Collection); Dorothy Seay Magoffin, "A Georgia Planter and His Plantations, 1837–1861," *North Carolina Historical Review*, XV (October, 1938), 376; Sydnor, *A Gentleman of the Old Natchez Region*, 103; J. Carlyle Sitterson, *Sugar Country: The Cane Sugar Indus-*

try in the South, 1753–1950 (Lexington, 1953), 98–99; Sir Charles Lyell, A Second Visit to North America, 2 Vols. (New York, 1849), I, 264–65; Caldwell, "Christmas in Old Natchez," 261.

24. Sitterson, Sugar Country, 98; slave figures from MS census returns, 1840, 1850 (Microfilm copies in Louisiana State University Library), St. James Parish, Louisiana; Caldwell, "Christmas in Old Natchez," 261.

25. Sitterson, Sugar Country, 99.

26. Lyell, A Second Visit to North America, I, 268.

27. Killona Plantation Journals (MSS in Mississippi Department of Archives and History, Jackson), July 20, 1841; Theodora Britton Marshall and Gladys Crail Evans (eds.), "Plantation Report from the Papers of Levin R. Marshall, of 'Richmond,' Natchez, Mississippi," Journal of Mississippi History, III (January, 1941), 53; Deer Range Plantation Record (Maunsel White Papers and Books), August 29, 1853.

28. Martin Gordon, Jr., to Benjamin Tureaud, December 30, 1852, in Benjamin Tureaud Papers, Louisiana State University Department of Archives.

29. Record of Births and Deaths of Negroes, in Ashland Plantation Record Book (MS in Louisiana State University Department of Archives), 1852.

30. William D. Postell, The Health of Slaves on Southern Plantations (Baton Rouge, 1951), 164.

31. Bayside Plantation Records (Southern Historical Collection), I, March 24, 1848; Deer Range Plantation Record (Maunsel White Papers and Books), June 21, 1852; Southern Cultivator, X (August, 1852), 227.

32. For examples in the latter category, see M. D. Bringier in Account with Houmas Plantation, May 7, 1844, in Louis A. Bringier and Family Papers (MSS in Louisiana State University Department of Archives), I, 91; Account with Edmund Ruffin, September 25, 1850, in William Hartwell Macon Physicians Account Book (MS in Swem Library, William and Mary College, Williamsburg), 102. I am indebted to Sterling P. Anderson, Jr., of Upper Marlbourne, Virginia, for providing me with copies of pertinent sections in the latter source.

33. Evan Hall Plantation Account Books (Microfilm copy in Southern Historical Collection), January 1, 1825; Dr. B. F. Holcombe in Account with Thomas Butler, November 22, 1843, in Thomas Butler and Family Papers (MSS in Louisiana State University Department of Archives); Sydnor, A Gentleman of the Old Natchez Region, 105.

34. Lyell, A Second Visit to North America, I, 264. I am indebted to James E. Bagwell, a professor at Georgia Southwestern College and a doctoral student of mine, for making available to me this and other items pertaining to Couper.

35. Westover Plantation Journal (Southern Historical Collection), August 9, 31, 1860; Thomas Butler to Ann Butler, March 21, 1846, Thomas Butler and Family Papers.

36. Deer Range Plantation Journal (Maunsel White Papers and Books), IV–VI.

37. Riley (ed.), "Diary of a Mississippi Planter," 450.

38. Moore Rawls to Lewis Thompson, June 25, 1857, in Lewis Thompson Papers, Southern Historical Collection.

39. Maunsel White to W. H. Scott, January 3, 1849, Maunsel White Lettercopy Book, in Maunsel White Papers and Books.

40. William G. Wright to Lewis Thompson, November 20, 1860, Lewis Thompson Papers.

Notes

176 Notes

41. Genovese, *Roll, Jordan, Roll*, 293.

42. Hill Carter, "On the Management of Negroes," *Farmers' Register*, I (February, 1834), 564.

43. Rules and Regulations for the Government of Waterloo, Southdown, and Hollywood Plantations, in William J. Minor Plantation Diaries (MSS in William J. Minor and Family Papers, Louisiana State University Department of Archives), XXXIII (1861–65), XXXIV (1861–68).

44. Magoffin, "A Georgia Planter and His Plantations," 374; Ulrich B. Phillips (ed.), *Plantation and Frontier Documents, 1649–1863*, 2 Vols. (Cleveland, 1909), I, 118.

45. Ulrich B. Phillips, *American Negro Slavery* (New York, 1918), 283.

46. The following sketch is based upon material in the Maunsel White Papers and Books, Southern Historical Collection. For additional information on White, see Clement Eaton, "The Commercial Mind: The New Orleans Merchant Maunsel White," in *The Mind of the Old South* (Baton Rouge, 1964), 43–60.

47. Deer Range Plantation Journal (Maunsel White Papers and Books), December 26, 1858; Maunsel White to James N. Bracewell, May 17, 1848; January 21, 1849, Maunsel White Lettercopy Book, in Maunsel White Papers and Books. Italics added by author.

48. Maunsel White to Maunsell White, Jr., July 14, 1860; Deer Range Plantation Record, October 20, 1852; Deer Range Plantation Journal, December 18, 1856; August 16, 1860; May 7, 1861, all in Maunsel White Papers and Books.

49. Fogel and Engerman, *Time on the Cross*, 145.

50. The following evaluation of Barrow is based upon diary entries published in Davis, *Plantation Life in Louisiana*.

51. Davis, *Plantation Life in Louisiana*, 214.

52. *Ibid.*, 183, 329, 242.

53. Richard D. Powell to John Hartwell Cocke, January 23, 1864, in Cocke Papers, Southern Historical Collection.

54. John M. Witherspoon to Peter Wilson Hairston, March 8, 1853, in Peter Wilson Hairston Papers, XXI, Southern Historical Collection.

55. Thomas Butler to Ann Butler, July 22, 1842, Thomas Butler and Family Papers.

56. John Berkley Grimball Diary (MS in Southern Historical Collection), October 12, 17, 20, 1832.

57. Carter, "On the Management of Negroes," 565.

58. For examples, see *De Bow's Review*, XXVI (May, 1859), 579; Phillips (ed.), *Plantation and Frontier Documents*, I, 113.

59. Postell, *Health of Slaves*, 24–25.

60. Richard D. Powell to John Hartwell Cocke, July 19, 1856, Cocke Papers; H. M. Seale Diary (MS in Louisiana State University Department of Archives), January 10, 1853.

61. Moore Rawls to Lewis Thompson, April 9, 1858, Lewis Thompson Papers.

62. Scarborough (ed.), *Diary of Edmund Ruffin*, I, 250; II, 554.

63. Genovese, *Roll, Jordan, Roll*, 591. See also Genovese's forthcoming monograph, *Afro-American Slave Revolts in the Making of the Modern World*.

64. For example, see Moore Rawls to Lewis Thompson, October 3, 1858, Lewis Thompson Papers.

65. Scarborough (ed.), *Diary of Edmund Ruffin*, II, 208.

66. Stephen Duncan to Thomas Butler, October 4, 1831, Thomas Butler and Family Papers.
67. *Niles' Register*, XLIX (January 16, 1836), 331.
68. Scarborough (ed.), *Diary of Edmund Ruffin*, I, 482.
69. Grimball Diary (Southern Historical Collection), December 17, 1860.
70. Stephen Duncan to Thomas Butler, July 1, 1823, Thomas Butler and Family Papers.
71. Scarborough (ed.), *Diary of Edmund Ruffin*, II, 346, 470–71.
72. Manigault Plantation Records (MSS in Southern Historical Collection), IV, June 12, 1862.
73. Alexander Franklin Pugh Plantation Diaries (MSS in Louisiana State University Department of Archives), November 20, 26, 1862.
74. Clement Eaton, *A History of the Old South: The Emergence of a Reluctant Nation* (New York, 1975), 3.
75. Scarborough (ed.), *Diary of Edmund Ruffin*, II, 357–58.

Notes to SLAVERY—THE HISTORIAN'S BURDEN
by Kenneth M. Stampp

1. Robert McColley, *Slavery and Jeffersonian Virginia* (Urbana, 1964), 2–3.
2. Winthrop D. Jordan, *White Over Black* (Chapel Hill, 1968), 342, 374.
3. These obstacles are discussed fully in David Brion Davis, *The Problem of Slavery in the Age of the Revolution, 1770–1823* (Ithaca, N.Y., 1975). See especially Chapters 1–4 and pp. 255–62.
4. South Carolina, after closing the trade in 1787, reopened it in 1803 and kept it open until it was closed in 1808 by an act of Congress.
5. For the role of Quakers in the early antislavery movement see Davis, *The Problem of Slavery in the Age of Revolution*, Chapter 5.
6. Robert William Fogel and Stanley L. Engerman, *Time on the Cross* (Boston, 1974), I, 226.
7. *Ibid.*, 4–6, 8.
8. George Fitzhugh, *Cannibals All! or, Slaves Without Masters* (Richmond, 1857), 31.
9. Thomas R. Dew, *A Review of the Debate in the Virginia Legislature of 1831 and 1832* (Richmond, 1832).
10. Dew, *Review*, quoted in Washington, D.C. *Political Register*, October 16, 1833, p. 790.
11. E. N. Elliott (ed.), *Cotton Is King: and Pro-Slavery Arguments* (Augusta, Ga., 1860), 538.
12. Fogel and Engerman, *Time on the Cross*, I, 3.
13. Eugene D. Genovese, *Roll, Jordan, Roll: The World the Slaves Made* (New York, 1974).
14. Fogel and Engerman, *Time on the Cross*, I, 4.
15. Genovese, *Roll, Jordan, Roll*, xvi.
16. See Thomas L. Haskell, "The True and Tragical History of *Time on the Cross*," *New York Review of Books* (October 2, 1975), 33–39.
17. See Eugene D. Genovese, *The World the Slaveholders Made* (New York, 1969), *passim*.

18. Stanley Engerman in Alfred H. Conrad et al., "Slavery As an Obstacle to Economic Growth in the United States: A Panel Discussion," *Journal of Economic History*, XXVII (December, 1967), 542.

19. Jane H. Pease, "A Note on Patterns of Conspicuous Consumption Among Seaboard Planters, 1820–1860," *Journal of Southern History*, XXXV (August, 1969), 381–93.

20. Allan Nevins and Milton Halsey Thomas (eds.), *The Diary of George Templeton Strong, 1835–1875*, (New York, 1952).

21. Ulrich B. Phillips, *Life and Labor in the Old South* (New York, 1929), 196; Herbert Aptheker, *American Negro Slave Revolts* (New York, 1943), 374; Stanley M. Elkins, *Slavery: A Problem in American Institutional and Intellectual Life* (Chicago, 1968), 82; John W. Blassingame, *The Slave Community* (New York, 1972), 201.

22. Robert S. Starobin, *Blacks in Bondage: Letters of American Slaves* (New York, 1974).

23. Two chapters in Lawrence W. Levine's forthcoming book, *Black Culture and Black Consciousness*, explore the slave's culture and mind through his songs and folklore. See also his "Slave Songs and Slave Consciousness," in Tamara Hareven (ed.), *Anonymous Americans* (Englewood Cliffs, N. J., 1971), 99–126, and Sterling Stuckey, "Through the Prism of Folklore: Black Ethos in Slavery," *Massachusetts Review*, IX (Summer 1968), 417–37.

24. See George P. Rawick (ed.), *The American Slave: A Composite Autobiography*, (Westport, Conn., 1972).

25. John W. Blassingame, in "Using the Testimony of Ex-Slaves: Approaches and Problems," *Journal of Southern History*, XLI (November, 1975), 473–92, makes some acute observations on the limitations of the slave narratives, which he did not use in his book, *The Slave Community* (New York, 1972). He is decidedly less acute in his critique of the autobiographies, which he *did* use.

Bibliographical Essay

Several times during the last quarter of a century historians have suggested that the study of slavery had reached its natural limits. In 1947, Allan Nevins, the major synthesizer of mid-nineteenth century history, attempted to close the debates, and twenty years later David M. Potter, one of the more eminent historians of the South, suggested that the study of slavery had reached the point of diminishing returns.[1] And yet the literature since 1967 has been voluminous; indeed, more than a dozen highly significant books on slavery were published during 1974–75. Because the bibliography of slavery is so immense and has been augmented to such a degree during the last few years, a short introduction or overview of the recent scholarship may prove helpful to students.[2]

1. Allan Nevins, *Ordeal of the Union* (New York: Charles Scribner's Sons, 1947), I, 412–544; Stanley M. Elkins, *Slavery: A Problem in American Institutional and Intellectual Life* (2nd ed.; Chicago: University of Chicago Press, 1968), 24; David M. Potter, "Depletion and Renewal in Southern History," in Edgar T. Thompson, ed., *Perspectives on the South: Agenda for Research* (Durham: Duke University Press, 1967), 78–79.
    2. For historiographical essays dealing with slavery see James C. Bonner, "Plantation and Farm: The Agricultural South," and Bennett H. Wall, "African Slavery," in Arthur S. Link and Rembert W. Patrick, eds., *Writing Southern History: Essays in Historiography in Honor of Fletcher M. Green* (Baton Rouge: Louisiana State University Press, 1965), 147–97; Eugene D. Genovese, foreword, "Ulrich Bonnell Phillips & His Critics," in Ulrich Bonnell Phillips, *American Negro Slavery* (2nd paperback ed.; Baton Rouge: Louisiana State University Press, 1969), vii–xxi; Allen Weinstein and Frank Otto Gatell, *American Negro Slavery: A Modern Reader* (2nd ed.; New York: Oxford University Press, 1973), which contains an excellent bibliography; James W. McPherson, Laurence B. Holland, James M. Banner, Jr., Nancy J. Weiss, and Michael D. Bell, eds., *Blacks in*

Ulrich Bonnell Phillips' *American Negro Slavery* (1918) served almost two generations of students. While his seminal ideas dominated the field, historians tended to concentrate on a rather narrow perspective which included the morality of slavery, agricultural operations, plantation management, conditions within slavery, the planter class, and the economics of slavery. Although a "perennial debate" concerning the profitability of slavery flourished, consensus on many other aspects of slavery was almost assured.[3] Early opposition to Phillips' views by such historians as Carter G. Woodson, W. E. B. Du Bois, and Herbert Aptheker was largely ignored. During the critical years of the 1930s and 1940s, sociologists Gunnar Myrdal, Melville Herskovits, and E. Franklin Frazier joined the dissenting historians in offering challenges and new viewpoints. The increasing dissatisfaction with Phillips' traditional view culminated in Kenneth M. Stampp's *The Peculiar Institution: Slavery in the Ante-Bellum South*, published in 1956. Stampp's scholarship was the much needed counterweight to the traditional view, and *The Peculiar Institution* is correctly regarded as a major turning point in the historiography of slavery. While Professor Stampp's work should not be minimized, another study appeared just three years after *The Peculiar Institution*, and presented such subtle, novel, and sophisticated conceptualizations that practically all subsequent writings about slavery are, in varying degrees, indebted to it. Stanley M. Elkins' *Slavery: A Problem in American Institutional and Intellectual Life* (1959) generated heated debates which have shaped the historiography of slavery to the present.

Elkins' *Slavery* was responsible for much of the literature on slavery since 1960. It would be foolhardy to argue that each writer consciously attempted to refute (or to support) a particular point found in Elkins' study, but it is suggested that the historiography of the last decade and a half may be divided into three broad

America: Bibliographical Essays (New York: Doubleday and Company, 1971), containing excellent essays on black American history. See also David Brion Davis, "Slavery and the Post-World War II Historians," *Daedalus*, CIII (Spring, 1974), 1–16.

3. C. Vann Woodward, "Clio with Soul," *Journal of American History*, LVI (June, 1969), 5–20.

categories, each of which was generated by Elkins' original work. The comparison of slavery in the southern United States with other regions of the New World formed the first of the three categories. The second concerned the problem of culture and the impact of the environment on slaves and their responses to it; this produced the greatest response which focused on countering the "Sambo" image and in examining plantation environments to determine the range of alternatives open to slaves. The final category concerned slavery and the American mind: the southern defense of and the abolitionists' attacks on slavery—old arguments which have been enhanced by new insights.

Elkins' assumptions regarding the happy, docile, and contented Sambo and his analogy of slavery in the southern United States with the Nazi concentration camps of World War II drew immediate rejoinders, which have been admirably treated in *The Debate over Slavery: Stanley Elkins and His Critics* (1971), edited by Ann J. Lane, and in an article by Kenneth M. Stampp, "Rebels and Sambos: The Search for the Negro's Personality in Slavery," *Journal of Southern History* (XXXVII, 1971). Elkins' methodology and the Sambo image need no further comment here.[4] It is significant, however, to emphasize that most of the later work in slavery was directly or indirectly generated by Elkins' controversial study.

The scholarship that was influenced by Elkins' methodology in comparing slavery in the United States with Latin American slavery, while continuing, has abated somewhat in the last few years. Assuming Latin American slavery to have been less harsh (or at least containing greater ameliorating influences) than slavery in the United States, Elkins revived and expanded on the seminal essay of Frank Tannenbaum, *Slave and Citizen: The Negro in the Americas* (1946). David Brion Davis expressed the opposing view in his prize-winning book *The Problem of Slavery in Western Culture* (1966), the first volume in a projected three-volume study of the abolitionist movement. Soon the cliometricians reported

4. Stanley M. Elkins, "Slavery and Ideology," in Ann J. Lane, ed., *The Debate over Slavery: Stanley Elkins and His Critics* (Urbana: University of Illinois Press, 1971), 325–26.

significant findings, especially Philip D. Curtin in his study *The Atlantic Slave Trade: A Census* (1969), which dramatically compared the number of slaves imported into various areas of the New World. Utilizing the comparative approach, such studies as Herbert S. Klein's *Slavery in the Americas: A Comparative Study of Cuba and Virginia* (1971) and Franklin W. Knight's *Slavery in Cuba During the Nineteenth Century* (1971) reflected the methodology and questions raised by Elkins. There are several excellent studies of Brazilian slavery, but Carl N. Degler, using the comparative method in *Neither White Nor Black: Slavery and Race Relations in Brazil and the United States* (1971), maintained that slaves in the United States constituted the only slave society in either the ancient or modern systems that expanded through natural increase rather than by increased importations. This theme is expressed as part of the irony of American slavery in the first essay in this volume. David M. Cohen and Jack P. Green, in *Neither Slave Nor Free: The Freedmen of African Descent in the Slave Societies of the New World* (1972), expanded on the comparative approach by considering social groups other than slaves. *Slavery, Colonialism, and Racism* (1974), edited by Sidney W. Mintz, is a reprint of the Spring issue of *Daedalus* (CIII, 1974). Ann M. Pescatello's *The African in Latin America* (1975) is an outstanding compilation of essays concerning slavery in Latin America and includes a useful bibliographical essay.[5]

Stanley Elkins' concept of the closed society and the authoritarian system of slavery in the southern United States raised the issue of acculturation and slave responses, which generated the second category in recent historiography. The scholarly (and sometimes not so scholarly) reaction to Elkins' study was enormous. Responding not only to his thesis but also to the presentism of the civil rights movement of the 1960s, students of slavery sought to counter the Sambo thesis and to correct the omissions of American history written by white historians by republishing long

---

5. See also Laura Foner and Eugene D. Genovese, eds., *Slavery in the New World: A Reader in Comparative History* (Englewood Cliffs: Prentice-Hall, Inc., 1969).

out of print sources.[6] The biographies and autobiographies of the fugitive slaves published in inexpensive paper editions offered students easy access to personal views of slavery. In addition, the collections of the Federal Writers Project, in which hundreds of former slaves were interviewed, have been published in several forms, the most significant being the multivolume *The American Slave: A Composite Autobiography* (1972), edited by George P. Rawick. Volume 1 of this series, *From Sundown to Sunup: The Making of the Black Community*, was the editor's narrative taken primarily from the interviews; Volumes 18 and 19 contained similar material preserved at Fisk University. While there are many published collections of documents pertaining to slavery, the most recent at this publishing was *A Documentary History of Slavery in North America* (1976), edited by Willie Lee Rose, which is valuable not only for her selection of documents, but also for her essay on sources and manuscript collections. John W. Blassingame has compiled a private collection of letters and documents which will soon be published. Students using the slave sources should see C. Vann Woodward, "History from Slave Sources," *American Historical Review* (LXXIX, 1974), for an evaluation of the interviews as primary sources.

Other efforts to counter the Sambo image included a great variety of articles and monographs, ranging from John Henrik Clarke's collection of essays, *William Styron's Nat Turner: Ten Black Writers Respond* (1966), to scores of articles dealing with black folklore, songs, religion, day-to-day resistance, and slave revolts. Several of the significant monographs include Larry Gara, *The Liberty Line: The Legend of the Underground Railroad* (1961), and Gerald W. Mullin, *Flight and Rebellion: Slave Resistance in Eighteenth Century Virginia* (1972). John W. Blassingame's admirable use of the often ignored fugitive slave biographies, the slave narratives of the Federal Writers Project, and his private collection of letters offered new insights into slave

6. For a discussion of presentism and historians see Davis, "Slavery and the Post-World War II Historians," 7–13, and David H. Donald's review of Eugene D. Genovese, *Roll, Jordan, Roll: The World the Slaves Made*, in *Commentary*, LIX (January, 1975), 86–90.

responses to bondage. He listed the most significant sources in the bibliography to his study *The Slave Community: Plantation Life in the Ante-Bellum South* (1972). Examining the slave responses, which ranged along a continuum from accommodation to rebellion, Blassingame stressed the strength of the slave family and the slaves who not only defended and provided for their families, but also maintained their own sense of identity and self-worth even while remaining in bondage. Professor Blassingame interpreted the slaves' concept of the community's social structure in a paper which is included in this volume.

Eugene D. Genovese's monumental scholarship in *Roll, Jordan, Roll: The World the Slaves Made* (1974) is one of the more significant recent contributions to the study of slavery. Genovese's study marked a major turning point in historiography, which for the last fifteen years has reflected the influence of Elkins. Where previous writers, even with the best of intentions, attempted to offset the Sambo image, Genovese established the construct for recognizing the dual structure of the institution. His discussion of paternalism, though needing elaboration, offered a subtle perspective for examining slave responses. While Elkins' three explanations for slave responses—infantilism, substitution of significant others for self, and role-playing—involved or even required internalization to some degree, Genovese's concept of paternalism has made it possible to analyze slave responses in more realistic terms. In the preface to *Roll, Jordan, Roll*, he stated that "slavery . . . made white and black southerners one people while making them two," and that "an understanding of the slaves requires some understanding of the masters and others who helped shape a complex society. Masters and slaves shaped each other and cannot be discussed or analyzed in isolation."[7] Genovese summarized the slaveholders' sense of paternalism as a "duty and a burden." Yet this paternalism recognized the humanity of the slave, and "the slaves found an opportunity to translate paternalism itself into a doctrine different from that understood by

---

7. Eugene D. Genovese, *Roll, Jordan, Roll: The World the Slaves Made* (New York: Pantheon Books, 1974), xvi–xvii.

their masters and to forge it into a weapon of resistance to assertions that slavery was a natural condition for blacks, that blacks were racially inferior, and that black slaves had no rights or legitimate claims of their own."[8] Accepting paternalism as the mechanism whereby planters maintained hegemony over the slaves, he also posited paternalism as a method whereby slaves could maintain and even demand limts to their servitude. Genovese used black drivers, black ministers, and other groups to a lesser degree to illustrate slave responses that ranged from accommodation to resistance within the paternalistic construct. While many other writers used the accommodation-resistance continuum, Genovese placed it in context of the complex relationship between masters and slaves. It would be surprising if Professor Genovese's subtle analysis does not dominate the historiography of the coming decade.

To comprehend more fully the master-slave relationships required further analysis of the socioeconomic system. Several works by Genovese are recognized as contributing to perspectives on slavery, especially his study *The Political Economy of Slavery: Studies in the Economy and Society of the Slave South* (1961); these ideas were expanded and revised in his *The World the Slaveholders Made: Two Essays in Interpretation* (1969). New directions in the economy of slavery were pointed out in Robert S. Starobin's *Industrial Slavery in the Old South* (1970) and in Richard Wade's *Slavery in the Cities: The South 1820–1860* (1964). However, almost all discussions of the slave economy must consider market functions and profitability. James C. Bonner's historiographical essay "Plantation and Farm: The Agricultural South," published in *Writing Southern History* (1965), adequately recognized the earlier studies in plantation management, and Harold D. Woodman surveyed the literature in an incisive article, "The Profitability of Slavery: A Historical Perennial," *Journal of Southern History* (XXIX, 1963). The profitability of slavery cannot be discussed without reference to Alfred H. Conrad and John R. Meyer, whose original article "The Economics of Slavery in the

8. *Ibid.*, 7.

Ante-Bellum South,"*Journal of Political Economy* (LXVI, 1958), helped establish the econometric methodology. This article, reprinted many times, was also included in a collection of the more important articles on the economics of slavery in *Did Slavery Pay?: Readings in the Economics of Black Slavery in the United States*, edited by Hugh G. J. Aitken in 1971. Certainly the most controversial examination of the slave economy was the recently published *Time on the Cross: The Economics of American Negro Slavery* (1974) and its supplementary volume, *Time on the Cross: Evidence and Methods* (1974), by Robert W. Fogel and Stanley L. Engerman.

Professors Fogel and Engerman, writing in their prologue "Slavery and the Cliometric Revolution," noted that a "vast literature has accumulated" and, even while students of slavery disagreed, "a broad consensus" has emerged. They claimed that the methodology and new sources of the cliometricians had "contradicted many of the most important propositions in the traditional portrayal of the slave system." Listing ten topics, the authors pointed out what they believed to be the traditional views and added their new interpretations.[9] For the student who has kept pace with the literature regarding slavery, Fogel and Engerman hardly presented new interpretations. Kenneth Stampp's essay in the present volume discusses the interpretations in *Time on the Cross*. Furthermore, two significant analyses of *Time on the Cross*—Herbert Gutman's *Slavery and the Numbers Game: A Critique of "Time on the Cross"* (1975), and a collaborative effort entitled *Reckoning with Slavery: Critical Essays in the Quantitative History of American Negro Slavery* (1976), containing essays by Paul A. David, Herbert G. Gutman, Richard Sutch, Peter Temin, Gavin Wright, and Kenneth Stampp—reflect most of the present thought regarding the errors, omissions, and shortcomings of *Time on the Cross*. But the contribution of the cliometricians should not be dismissed lightly, for they raised questions regarding the slave family, conditions within slavery, the produc-

9. Robert W. Fogel and Stanley L. Engerman, *Time on the Cross: The Economics of American Negro Slavery* (Boston: Little, Brown and Company, 1974), 3–6.

tivity of slave labor, and the function of markets in the southern slave economy. It is conceivable that Fogel and Engerman have done for the economics of slavery what Elkins did for the study of slave personality. If such is the case, *Time on the Cross* will join with *Roll, Jordan, Roll* in representing new trends in the historiography of slavery.

The third question raised by Stanley Elkins concerned the role of intellectuals and institutions in the abolitionist movement. The scholarly response to this problem has been less than that devoted to slave culture and personality. Nevertheless, significant studies have been made and include biographies and monographs examining slavery and the American mind. Several historiographical essays may be suggested: Richard O. Curry, "Abolitionists and Reconstruction: A Critical Appraisal," *Journal of Southern History* (XXXIV, 1968); Merton L. Dillon, "The Abolitionists: A Decade of Controversy, 1959–1969," *Journal of Southern History* (XXXV, 1969); and Martin Duberman, *The Anti-Slavery Vanguard: New Essays on the Abolitionists* (1965). Gerald Sorin in *Abolitionism: A New Perspective* (1972) attempted to synthesize the recent literature on the abolitionists, and his work includes a useful bibliography. James M. McPherson viewed the abolitionist movement as continuing the spirit of reform into the Reconstruction period in his study *The Struggle for Equality: Abolitionists and the Negro in the Civil War and Reconstruction* (1964), and Benjamin Quarles presented a long-neglected aspect of the abolitionists in his volume *Black Abolitionists* (1969). Bertram Wyatt-Brown, *Lewis Tappan and the Evangelical War Against Slavery* (1969), offered a sympathetic narrative of the activities of an influential abolitionist, while Aileen Kraditor in *Means and Ends in American Abolitionism: Garrison and His Critics on Strategy and Tactics, 1834–1850* (1969) broadened the perspective by examining the ideas and emotions of the abolitionists. Merton L. Dillon sought to portray the differences between various abolitionist groups and their changing relations with political activities in his study *The Abolitionists: The Growth of a Dissenting Minority* (1974).

Eugene D. Genovese interpreted the southern perspective in

188 Bibliographical Essay

The World the Slaveholders Made: Two Essays in Interpretation (1969) by examining the pro-slavery arguments of George Fitzhugh and the hegemony of the slaveowning class. William K. Scarborough's scholarly edition of *The Diary of Edmund Ruffin* (I, 1972; II, 1976) admirably reflected the views of a major southern fire-eater, and Mary Frances Berry, *Black Resistance/White Law: A Constitutional History of Racism in America* (1971), devoted her first seven chapters to the political and legal systems and slavery.

Winthrop D. Jordan, in his excellent study *White Over Black: American Attitudes Toward the Negro, 1550–1812* (1968), analyzed the origins of racism and its continuing influence on the thought of white America, while George Frederickson continued the portrayal of racism in America, including the racial ambivalence of the abolitionists, in *The Black Image in the White Mind: The Debate on Afro-American Character and Destiny, 1817–1914* (1971). The monumental undertaking of David Brion Davis was two-thirds completed with the publication of his two volumes *The Problem of Slavery in Western Culture* (1966) and *The Problem of Slavery in the Age of Revolution, 1770–1823* (1975). The first volume considered the distinctions between ancient and modern slavery and between slavery in the United States and Latin America, as well as abolitionist thought among religious groups through the Age of the Enlightenment. The second volume emphasized abolitionism in England and early abolitionist efforts in the United States. When completed, Davis' study of the abolitionist movement may join *Roll, Jordan, Roll* and *Time on the Cross* as major turning points in writing the history of American Negro slavery.

The preceding paragraphs have not attempted to present a bibliography of slavery, but to offer a broad overview of the last fifteen years. While Elkins' *Slavery* provided the conceptualizations which formed the basis of the writings during those years, it is suggested that additional concepts have emerged to give new directions in interpreting slavery. Eugene Genovese's concept of paternalism, the questions raised by *Time on the Cross*, and the meticulous examination of abolitionism by David Brion Davis could well form the basis for the historiography of the next fifteen years.

DATE DUE

DISPLAY			
FEB 8 '89			
FEB 2 1983			
I 11 7-15-88 DE 20 '89			
NOV 3 0			
NOV 3 0			
DE 04 '93			
DEC 1 5 1997			
APR 0 3			
APR 3 1998			
GAYLORD			PRINTED IN U.S.A.